CURIOSITIES OF P꜀ ꜀꜀ꞏꞏꞏ NOMENCLATURE

BY

Charles Wareing Endell Bardsley

CURIOSITIES OF PURITAN NOMENCLATURE

Published by Dossier Press

New York City, NY

First published circa 1898

Copyright © Dossier Press, 2015

All rights reserved

ABOUT DOSSIER PRESS

Since the moment people have been writing, they've been writing non-fiction works, from the *Histories* of Herodotus to the Code of Hammurabi. **Dossier Press** publishes all of the classic non-fiction works ever written and makes them available to new and old readers alike at the touch of a button.

CURIOSITIES OF PURITAN NOMENCLATURE

By the same Author.

Crown 8vo, cloth extra, 7s. 6d.

OUR ENGLISH SURNAMES: their Sources and Significations.

"Mr. Bardsley has faithfully consulted the original mediæval documents and works from which the origin and development of surnames can alone be satisfactorily traced. He has furnished a valuable contribution to the literature of surnames, and we hope to hear more of him in this field."—Times.

CHATTO AND WINDUS, PICCADILLY, W.

CURIOSITIES

OF

PURITAN NOMENCLATURE

BY

CHARLES W. BARDSLEY

AUTHOR OF "ENGLISH SURNAMES, THEIR SOURCES AND SIGNIFICATIONS"

London

CHATTO AND WINDUS, PICCADILLY

1880

[The right of translation is reserved]

Printed by William Clowes and Sons, Limited, London and Beccles.

DEDICATED TO

HIS FELLOW MEMBERS

OF THE

HARLEIAN SOCIETY.

PREFACE.

I will not be so ill-natured as to quote the names of all the writers who have denied the existence of Puritan eccentricities at the font. One, at least, ought to have known better, for he has edited more books of the Puritan epoch than any other man in England. The mistake of all is that, misled perhaps by Walter Scott and Macaulay, they have looked solely to the Commonwealth period. The custom was then in its decay.

I have to thank several clergymen for giving me extracts from the registers and records under their care. A stranger to them, I felt some diffidence in making my requests. In every case the assistance I asked for was readily extended. These gentlemen are the Rev. W. Sparrow Simpson, St. Matthew, Friday Street, London; the Rev. W. Wodehouse, Elham, Canterbury; the Rev. J. B. Waytes, Markington, Yorks.; the Rev. William Tebbs, Caterham Valley; the Rev. Canon Howell, Drayton, Norwich; the Rev. J. O. Lord, Northiam, Staplehurst; and the Rev. G. E. Haviland, Warbleton, Sussex. The last-named gentleman copied no less than 120 names, all of Puritan origin, from the Warbleton records. I beg to thank him most warmly, and to congratulate him on possessing the most remarkable register of its kind in England. Certain circumstances led me to suspect that Warbleton was a kind of head-quarters of these eccentricities; I wrote to the rector, and we soon found that we had "struck ile." That Mr. Heley, the Puritan incumbent, should have baptized his own children by such names as Fear-not and Much-mercy, was not strange, but that he should have persuaded the majority of his parishioners to follow his example proves wonderful personal influence.

Amongst the laity, I owe gratitude to Mr. Chaloner Smith, Richmond, Surrey; Mr. R. R. Lloyd, St. Albans; Mr. J. E. Bailey, F.S.A., Manchester; Mr. J. L. Beardsley, Cleveland, U.S.A.; Mr. Tarbutts, Cranbrook, Kent; and Mr. Speed, Ulverston.

Of publications, I must needs mention Notes and Queries, a treasure-house to all antiquaries; the Sussex Archæological Society's works, and the Yorkshire Archæological and Topographical Journal. The "Wappentagium de Strafford" of the latter is the best document yet published for students of nomenclature. Out of it alone a complete history of English surnames and baptismal names might be written. Though inscribed with clerkly formality, it contained more pet forms than any other record I have yet seen; and this alone must stamp it as a most important document. The Harleian Society, by publishing church registers, have set a good example, and I have made much use of those that have been issued. They contain few instances of Puritan extravagance, but that is owing to the fact that no leading Puritan was minister of any of the three churches whose records they have so far printed. I sincerely hope the list of subscribers to this society may become enlarged.

For the rest—the result of twelve years' research—I am alone responsible. Heavy clerical responsibilities have often been lightened by a holiday spent among the yellow parchments of churches in town and country, from north to south of England. As it is possible I have seen as many registers as any other man in the country, I will add one statement—a very serious one: there are thousands of entries, at this moment faintly legible, which in another generation will be wholly illegible. What is to be done?

Should this little work meet the eye of any of the clergy in Sussex, Kent, and, I may add, Surrey, I would like to state that if they will search the baptismal records of the churches under their charge, say from 1580 to 1620, and furnish me with the result, I shall be very much obliged.

Vicarage, Ulverston,

March, 1880.

NOTE.

W. D. S. in the Prologue = "Wappentagium de Strafford."
C. S. P. = "Calendar of State Papers."
CONTENTS.
CURIOSITIES OF PURITAN NOMENCLATURE.

PROLOGUE.

THE PET-NAME EPOCH IN ENGLAND.

"One grows too fat, another too lean: modest Matilda, pretty pleasing Peg, sweet-singing Susan, mincing merry Moll, dainty dancing Doll, neat Nancy, jolly Joan, nimble Nell, kissing Kate, bouncing Bess with black eyes, fair Phillis with fine white hands, fiddling Frank, tall Tib, slender Sib, will quickly lose their grace, grow fulsome, stale, sad, heavy, dull, sour, and all at last out of fashion."—Anatomy of Melancholy.

"Be the jacks fair within, the jills fair without, the carpets laid, and everything in order?"—The Taming of the Shrew.

I. The Paucity of Names after the Conquest.

There were no Scripture names in England when the Conqueror took possession; even in Normandy they had appeared but a generation or two before William came over. If any are found in the old English period, we may feel assured they were ecclesiastic titles, adopted at ordination. Greek and Latin saints were equally unnoticed.

It is hard to believe the statement I have made. Before many generations had passed, Bartholomew, Simon, Peter, Philip, Thomas, Nicholas, John, and Elias, had engrossed a third of the male population; yet Domesday Book has no Philip, no Thomas, only one Nicholas, and but a sprinkling of Johns. It was not long before Jack and Jill took the place of Godric and Godgivu as representative of the English sexes, yet Jack was from the Bible, and Jill from the saintly Calendar.

Without entering into a deep discussion, we may say that the great mass of the old English names had gone down before the year 1200 had been reached. Those that survived only held on for bare existence. From the moment of William's advent, the names of the Norman began to prevail. He brought in Bible names, Saint names, and his own Teutonic names. The old English names bowed to them, and disappeared.

A curious result followed. From the year 1150 to 1550, four hundred years in round numbers, there was a very much smaller dictionary of English personal names than there had been for four hundred years before, and than there has been in the four hundred years since. The Norman list was really a small one, and yet it took possession of the whole of England.

A consequence of this was the Pet-name Epoch. In every community of one hundred Englishmen about the year 1300, there would be an average of twenty Johns and fifteen Williams; then would follow Thomas, Bartholomew, Nicholas, Philip, Simon, Peter, and Isaac from the Scriptures, and Richard, Robert, Walter, Henry, Guy, Roger, and Baldwin from the Teutonic list. Of female names, Matilda, Isabella, and Emma were first favourites, and Cecilia, Catharine, Margaret, and Gillian came closely upon their heels. Behind these, again, followed a fairly familiar number of names of either sex, some from the Teuton, some from the Hebrew, some from the Greek and Latin Church, but, when all told, not a large category.

It was, of course, impossible for Englishmen and Englishwomen to maintain their individuality on these terms. Various methods to secure a personality arose. The surname was adopted, and there were John Atte-wood, John the Wheelwright, John the Bigg, and John Richard's son, in every community. Among the middle and lower classes these did not become hereditary till so late as 1450 or 1500. This was not enough, for in common parlance it was not likely the full name would be used. Besides, there might be two, or even three, Johns in the same family. So late as March, 1545, the will of John Parnell de Gyrton runs:

"Alice, my wife, and Old John, my son, to occupy my farm together, till Olde John marries; Young John, my son, shall have Brenlay's land, plowed and sowed at Old John's cost."

The register of Raby, Leicestershire, has this entry:

"1559. Item: 29th day of August was John, and John Picke, the children of Xtopher and Anne, baptized.

"Item: the 31st of August the same John and John were buried."

Mr. Burns, who quotes these instances in his "History of Parish Registers," adds that at this same time "one John Barker had three sons named John Barker, and two daughters named Margaret Barker."

If the same family had but one name for the household, we may imagine the difficulty when this one name was also popular throughout the village. The difficulty was naturally solved by, firstly, the adoption of nick forms; secondly, the addition of pet desinences. Thus Emma became by the one practice simple Emm, by the other Emmott; and any number of boys in a small community might be entered in a register as Bartholomew, and yet preserve their individuality in work-a-day life by bearing such names as Bat, Bate, Batty, Bartle, Bartelot, Batcock, Batkin, and Tolly, or Tholy. In a word, these several forms of Bartholomew were treated as so many separate proper names.

No one would think of describing Wat Tyler's—we should now say Walter Tyler's—insurrection as Gowen does:

"Watte vocat, cui Thoma venit, neque Symme retardat,

Bat—que Gibbe simul, Hykke venire subent:

Colle furit, quem Bobbe juvat, nocumenta parantes,

Cum quibus, ad damnum Wille coire volat—

Crigge rapit, dum Davie strepit, comes est quibus Hobbe,

Larkin et in medio non minor esse putat:

Hudde ferit, quem Judde terit, dum Tibbe juvatur

Jacke domosque viros vellit, en ense necat."

These names, taken in order, are Walter, Thomas, Simon, Bartholomew, Gilbert, Isaac, Nicholas, Robert, William, Gregory, David, Robert (2), Lawrence, Hugh, Jordan (or George), Theobald, and John.

Another instance will be evidence enough. The author of "Piers Plowman" says—

"Then goeth Glutton in, and grete other after,

Cesse, the sonteresse, sat on the bench:

Watte, the warner, and his wife bothe:

Tymme, the tynkere, and twayne of his prentices:

Hikke, the hackney man, and Hugh, the pedlere,
Clarice, of Cokkeslane, and the clerke of the churche:
Dawe, the dykere, and a dozen othere."

Taken in their order, these nick forms represent Cecilia, Walter, Timothy, Isaac, Clarice, and David. It will be seen at a glance that such appellatives are rare, by comparison, in the present day. Tricks of this kind were not to be played with Bible names at the Reformation, and the new names from that time were pronounced, with such exceptions as will be detailed hereafter, in their fulness.

To speak of William and John is to speak of a race and rivalry 800 years old. In Domesday there were 68 Williams, 48 Roberts, 28 Walters, to 10 Johns. Robert Montensis asserts that in 1173, at a court feast of Henry II., Sir William St. John and Sir William Fitz-Hamon bade none but those who bore the name of William to appear. There were present 120 Williams, all knights. In Edward I.'s reign John came forward. In a Wiltshire document containing 588 names, 92 are William, 88 John, 55 Richard, 48 Robert, 23 Roger, Geoffrey, Ralph, and Peter 16. A century later John was first. In 1347, out of 133 common councilmen for London, first convened, 35 were John, 17 William, 15 Thomas, (St. Thomas of Canterbury was now an institution), 10 Richard, 8 Henry, 8 Robert. In 1385 the Guild of St. George at Norwich contained 377 names. Of these, John engrossed no less than 128, William 47, Thomas 41. The Reformation and the Puritan Commonwealth for a time darkened the fortunes of John and William, but the Protestant accession befriended the latter, and now, as 800 years ago, William is first and John second.

But when we come to realize that nearly one-third of Englishmen were known either by the name of William or John about the year 1300, it will be seen that the pet name and nick form were no freak, but a necessity. We dare not attempt a category, but the surnames of to-day tell us much. Will was quite a distinct youth from Willot, Willot from Wilmot, Wilmot from Wilkin, and Wilkin from Wilcock. There might be half a dozen Johns about the farmstead, but it mattered little so long as one was called Jack, another Jenning, a third Jenkin, a fourth Jackcock (now Jacox as a surname), a fifth Brownjohn, and a sixth Micklejohn, or Littlejohn, or Properjohn (i.e. well built or handsome).

The nick forms are still familiar in many instances, though almost entirely confined to such names as have descended from that day to the present. We still talk of Bob, and Tom, and Dick, and Jack. The introduction of Bible names at the Reformation did them much harm. But the Reformation, and the English Bible combined, utterly overwhelmed the pet desinences, and they succumbed. Emmot and Hamlet lived till the close of the seventeenth century, but only because they had ceased to be looked upon as altered forms of old favourite names, and were entered in vestry books on their own account as orthodox proper names.

II. Pet Forms.

These pet desinences were of four kinds.

(a) Kin.

The primary sense of kin seems to have been relationship: from thence family, or offspring. The phrases "from generation to generation," or "from father to son," in "Cursor Mundi" find a briefer expression:

"This writte was gett fra kin to kin,
That best it cuth to haf in min."

The next meaning acquired by kin was child, or "young one." We still speak in a diminutive sense of a manikin, kilderkin, pipkin, lambkin, jerkin, minikin (little minion), or doitkin. Appended to baptismal names it became very familiar. "A litul soth Sermun" says—

"Nor those prude yongemen
That loveth Malekyn,
And those prude maydenes
That loveth Janekyn:
....

Masses and matins
Ne kepeth they nouht,
For Wilekyn and Watekyn
Be in their thouht."

Unquestionably the incomers from Brabant and Flanders, whether as troopers or artisans, gave a great impulse to the desinence. They tacked it on to everything:

"Rutterkin can speke no Englyssh,
His tongue runneth all on buttyred fyssh,
Besmeared with grece abowte his dysshe
Like a rutter hoyda."

They brought in Hankin, and Han-cock, from Johannes; not to say Baudkin, or Bodkin, from Baldwin. Baudechon le Bocher in the Hundred Rolls, and Simmerquin Waller, lieutenant of the Castle of Harcourt in "Wars of the English in France," look delightfully Flemish.

Hankin is found late:

"Thus for her love and loss poor Hankin dies,
His amorous soul down flies."

"Musarum Deliciæ," 1655.

To furnish a list of English names ending in kin would be impossible. The great favourites were Hopkin (Robert), Lampkin and Lambkin (Lambert), Larkin (Lawrence), Tonkin (Antony), Dickin, Stepkin (Stephen), Dawkin (David), Adkin, now Atkin (Adam, not Arthur), Jeffkin (Jeffrey), Pipkin and Potkin (Philip), Simkin, Tipkin (Theobald), Tomkin, Wilkin, Watkin (Walter), Jenkin, Silkin (Sybil), Malkin (Mary), Perkin (Peter), Hankin (Hans), and Halkin or Hawkin (Henry). Pashkin or Paskin reminds us of Pask or Pash, the old baptismal name for children born at Easter. Judkin (now as a surname also Juckin) was the representative of Judd, that is, Jordan. George afterwards usurped the place. All these names would be entered in their orthodox baptismal style in all formal records. But here and there we get free and easy entries, as for instance:

"Agnes Hobkin-wyf, iiiid."—W. D. S.

"Henry, son of Halekyn, for 17½ acres of land."—"De Lacy Inquisition," 1311.

"Emma Watkyn-doghter, iiiid."—W. D. S.

"Thi beste cote, Hankyn,

Hath manye moles and spottes,

It moste ben y-wasshe."

"Piers Plowman."

Malkin was one of the few English female names with this appendage. Some relics of this form of Mary still remain. Malkin in Shakespeare is the coarse scullery wench:

"The kitchen malkin pins

Her richest lockram 'bout her reechy neck,

Clambering the walls to eye him."

"Coriolanus," Act ii. sc. 1.

While the author of the "Anatomy of Melancholy" is still more unkind, for he says—

"A filthy knave, a deformed quean, a crooked carcass, a maukin, a witch, a rotten post, a hedge-stake may be so set out and tricked up, that it shall make a fair show, as much enamour as the rest."—Part iii. sect. 2, mem. 2, sub-sect. 3.

From a drab Malkin became a scarecrow. Hence Chaucer talks of "malkin-trash." As if this were not enough, malkin became the baker's clout to clean ovens with. Thus, as Jack took the name of the implements Jack used, as in boot-jack, so by easy transitions Malkin. The last hit was when Grimalkin (that is, grey-malkin) came to be the cant term for an old worn-out quean cat. Hence the witch's name in "Macbeth."

It will be seen at a glance why Malkin is the only name of this class that has no place among our surnames. She had lost character. I have suggested, in "English Surnames," that Makin, Meakin, and Makinson owe their origin to either Mary or Maud. I would retract that supposition. There can be little doubt these are patronymics of Matthew, just as is Maycock or Meacock. Maykinus Lappyng occurs in "Materials for a History of Henry VII.," and the Maykina Parmunter of the Hundred Rolls is probably but a feminine form. The masculine name was often turned into a feminine, but I have never seen an instance of the reverse order.

Terminations in kin were slightly going down in popular estimation, when the Hebrew invasion made a clean sweep of them. They found shelter in Wales, however, and our directories preserve in their list of surnames their memorial for ever.

(b) Cock.

The term "cock" implied pertness: especially the pertness of lusty and swaggering youth. To cock up the eye, or the hat, or the tail, a haycock in a field, a cock-robin in the wood, and a cock-horse in the nursery, all had the same relationship of meaning—brisk action, pert demonstrativeness. The barn-door cockerel was not more cockapert than the boy in the scullery that opened upon the yard where both strutted. Hence any lusty lad was "Cock," while such fuller titles as Jeff-cock, or Sim-cock, or Bat-cock gave him a preciser individuality. The story of "Cocke Lorelle" is a relic of this; while the prentice lad in "Gammer Gurton's Needle," acted at Christ College, Cambridge, in 1566, goes by the only name of "Cock." Tib the servant wench says to Hodge, after the needle is gone—

"My Gammer is so out of course, and frantic all at once,

That Cock our boy, and I, poor wench, have felt it on our bones."

By-and-by Gammer calls the lad to search:

"Come hither, Cock: what, Cock, I say.

Cock.How, Gammer?

Gammer. Go, hie thee soon: and grope behind the old brass pan."

Such terms as nescock, meacock, dawcock, pillicock, or lobcock may be compounds—unless they owe their origin to "cockeney," a spoiled, home-cherished lad. In "Wit without Money" Valentine says—

"For then you are meacocks, fools, and miserable."

In "Appius and Virginia" (1563) Mausipula says (Act i. sc. 1)—

"My lady's great business belike is at end,

When you, goodman dawcock, lust for to wend."

In "King Lear"

"Pillicock sat on pillicock-hill"

seems an earlier rendering of the nursery rhyme—

"Pillicock, Pillicock sate on a hill,

If he's not gone, he sits there still."

In "Wily Beguiled" Will Cricket says to Churms—

"Why, since you were bumbasted that your lubberly legs would not carry your lobcock body."

These words have their value in proving how familiarly the term cock was employed in forming nicknames. That it should similarly be appended to baptismal names, especially the nick form of Sim, Will, or Jeff, can therefore present no difficulty.

Cock was almost as common as "kin" as a desinence. Sim-cock was Simcock to the end of his days, of course, if his individuality had come to be known by the name.

"Hamme, son of Adecock, held 29 acres of land.

"Mokock de la Lowe, for 10 acres.

"Mokock dal Moreclough, for six acres.

"Dik, son of Mocock, of Breercroft, for 20 acres."—"The De Lacy Inquisition," 1311.

Adecock is Adam, and Mocock or Mokock is Matthew. In the same way Sander-cock is a diminutive of Sander, Lay-cock of Lawrence, Luccock of Luke, Pidcock and Peacock of Peter, Maycock and Mycock of Matthew, Jeff-cock of Jeffrey, Johncock of John, Hitch-cock or Hiscock or Heacock of Higg or Hick (Isaac), Elcock of Ellis, Hancock or Handcock of Han or Hand (Dutch John), Drocock or Drewcock of Drew, Wilcock of William, Badcock or Batcock of Bartholomew, and Bawcock of Baldwin, Adcock or Atcock of Adam, Silcock of Silas, and Palcock of Paul:

"Johannes Palcock, et Beatrix uxor ejus, iiiid."—W. D. S.

"Ricardus Sylkok, et Matilda uxor ejus, iiiid."—W. D. S.

The difficulty of identification was manifestly lessened in a village or town where Bate could be distinguished from Batkin, and Batkin from Batcock. Hence, again, the common occurrence of such a component as cock. This diminutive is never seen in the seventeenth century; and yet we have many evidences of its use in the beginning of the sixteenth. The English Bible, with its tendency to require the full name as a matter of reverence, while it supplied new names in the place of the old ones that were accustomed to the desinence, caused this. It may be, too, that the new regulation of Cromwell in 1538, requiring the careful registration of all baptized children, caused parents to lay greater stress on the name as it was entered in the vestry-book.

Any way, the sixteenth century saw the end of names terminating in "cock."

(c.) On or In.

A dictionary instance is "violin," that is, a little viol, a fiddle of four strings, instead of six. This diminutive, to judge from the Paris Directory, must have been enormously popular with our neighbours. Our connection with Normandy and France generally brought the fashion to the English Court, and in habits of this kind the English folk quickly copied their superiors. Terminations in kin and cock were confined to the lower orders first and last. Terminations in on or in, and ot or et, were the introduction of fashion, and being under patronage of the highest families in the land, naturally obtained a much wider popularity.

Our formal registers, again, are of little assistance. Beton is coldly and orthodoxly Beatrice or Beatrix in the Hundred Rolls. Only here and there can we gather that Beatrice was never so called in work-a-day life. In "Piers Plowman" it is said—

"Beton the Brewestere
Bade him good morrow."

And again, later on:

"And bade Bette cut a bough,
And beat Betoun therewith."

If Alice is Alice in the registrar's hands, not so in homely Chaucer:

"This Alison answered: Who is there
That knocketh so? I warrant him a thefe."

Or take an old Yorkshire will:

"Item: to Symkyn, and Watkyn, and Alison Meek, servandes of John of Bolton, to ilk one of yaim, 26s. 8d."—"Test. Ebor." iii. 21. Surtees Society.

Hugh, too, gets his name familiarly entered occasionally:

"Hugyn held of the said earl an oxgang of land, and paid yearly iiis. vid."—"The De Lacy Inquisition," 1311.

Huggins in our directories is the memorial of this. But in the north of England Hutchin was a more popular form. In the "Wappentagium de Strafford" occurs—

"Willelmus Huchon, & Matilda uxor ejus, iiiid."

Also—

"Elena Houchon-servant, iiiid."

that is, Ellen the servant of Houchon. Our Hutchinsons are all north of Trent folk. Thus, too, Peter (Pier) became Perrin:

"The wife of Peryn."—"Manor of Ashton-under-Lyne," Chetham Society, p. 87.

Marion, from Mary, is the only familiar instance that has descended to us, and no doubt we owe this fact to Maid Marion, the May-lady. Many a Mary Ann, in these days of double baptismal names, perpetuates the impression that Marion or Marian was compounded of Mary and Ann.

Of familiar occurrence were such names as Perrin, from Pierre, Peter; Robin and Dobbin, from Rob and Dob, Robert; Colin, from Col, Nicholas; Diccon, from Dick, Richard; Huggin, from Hugh; Higgin, from Hick or Higg, Isaac; Figgin, from Figg, Fulke; Phippin, from Phip and Philip; and Gibbin, or Gibbon, or Gilpin, from Gilbert. Every instance proves the debt our surnames have incurred by this practice.

Several cases are obscured by time and bad pronunciation. Our Tippings should more rightly be Tippins, originally Tibbins, from Tibbe (Theobald); our Collinges and Collings, Collins; and our Gibbings, Gibbins. Our Jennings should be Jennins; Jennin Caervil was barber to the Earl of Suffolk in the French wars ("Wars of England in France," Henry VI.). Robing had early taken the place of Robin:

"Johanne Robyng-doghter, iiiid."—W. D. S.

Such entries as Raoulin Meriel and Raoul Partrer (this Raoul was private secretary to Henry VI.) remind us of the former popularity of Ralph and of the origin of our surnames Rawlins and Rawlinson:

"Dionisia Rawlyn-wyf, iiiid."—W. D. S.

Here again, however, the "in" has become "ing," for Rawlings is even more common than Rawlins. Deccon and Dickin have got mixed, and both are now Dickens, although Dicconson exists as distinct from Dickinson. Spenser knew the name well:

"Diggon Davie, I bid her 'good-day;'
Or Diggon her is, or I missay."

"Matilda Dicon-wyf, webester, iiiid."—W. D. S.

The London Directory contains Lamming and Laming. Alongside are Lampin, Lamin, and Lammin. These again are more correct, all being surnames formed from Lambin, a pet form of Lambert:

"Willelmus Lambyn, et Alicia uxor ejus, iiiid."—W. D. S.

Lambyn Clay played before Edward at Westminster at the great festival in 1306 (Chappell's "Popular Music of ye Olden Time," i. 29). The French forms are Lambin, Lamblin, and Lamberton, all to be met with in the Paris Directory.

All these names are relics of a custom that is obsolete in England, though not with our neighbours.

(d.) Ot and Et.

These are the terminations that ran first in favour for many generations.

This diminutive ot or et is found in our language in such words as poppet, jacket, lancet, ballot, gibbet, target, gigot, chariot, latchet, pocket, ballet. In the same way a little page became a paget, and hence among our surnames Smallpage, Littlepage, and Paget.

Coming to baptism, we find scarcely a single name of any pretensions to popularity that did not take to itself this desinence. The two favourite girl-names in Yorkshire previous to the Reformation were Matilda and Emma. Two of the commonest surnames there to-day are Emmott and Tillot, with such variations as Emmett and Tillett, Emmotson and Tillotson. The archbishop came from Yorkshire. Tyllot Thompson occurs under date 1414 in the "Fabric Rolls of York Minster" (Surtees Society).

"Rome, April 27, Eugenius IV. (1433). Dispensation from Selow for Richard de Akerode and Emmotte de Greenwood to marry, they being related in the fourth degree."—"Test. Ebor.," iii. 317.

"Licence to the Vicar of Bradford to marry Roger Prestwick and Emmote Crossley. Bannes thrice in one day" (1466).—"Test. Ebor.," iii. 338.

Isabella was also popular in Yorkshire: hence our Ibbots and Ibbotsons, our Ibbetts and Ibbetsons. Registrations such as "Ibbota filia Adam," or "Robert filius Ibote," are of frequent occurrence in the county archives. The "Wappentagium de Strafford" has:

"Johanna Ibot-doghter, iiiid.

"Willelmus Kene, et Ibota uxor ejus, iiiid.

"Thomas Gaylyour, et Ebbot sa femme, iiiid."

Cecilia became Sissot or Cissot:

"Willelmus Crake, & Cissot sa femme, iiiid."—W. D. S.

In the "Manor of Ashton-under-Lyne" (Chetham Society), penned fortunately for our purpose in every-day style, we have such entries as—

"Syssot, wife of Patrick.

"Syssot, wife of Diccon Wilson.

"Syssot, wife of Thomas the Cook.

"Syssot, wife of Jak of Barsley."

Four wives named Cecilia in a community of some twenty-five families will be evidence enough of the popularity of that name. All, however, were known in every-day converse as Sissot.

Of other girl-names we may mention Mabel, which from Mab became Mabbott; Douce became Dowcett and Dowsett; Gillian or Julian, from Gill or Jill (whence Jack and Jill), became Gillot, Juliet, and Jowett; Margaret became Margett and Margott, and in the north Magot. Hence such entries from the Yorkshire parchments, already quoted, as—

"Thomas de Balme, et Magota uxor ejus, chapman, iiiid.

"Hugo Farrowe, et Magota uxor ejus, smyth, iiiid.

"Johannes Magotson, iiiid."

Custance became Cussot, from Cuss or Cust, the nick form. The Hundred Rolls contain a "Cussot Colling"—a rare place to find one of these diminutives, for they are set down with great clerkly formality.

From Lettice, Lesot was obtained:

"Johan Chapman, & Lesot sa femme, iiiid."—W. D. S.

And Dionisia was very popular as Diot:

"Johannes Chetel, & Diot uxor ejus, iiiid.
"Willelmus Wege, & Diot uxor ejus, iiiid."—W. D. S.
Of course, it became a surname:
"Robertus Diot, & Mariona uxor ejus, iiiid.
"Willelmus Diotson, iiiid."—W. D. S.

It is curious to observe that Annot, which now as Annette represents Anne, in Richard II.'s day was extremely familiar as the diminutive of Annora or Alianora. So common was Annot in North England that the common sea-gull came to be so known. It is a mistake to suppose that Annot had any connection with Anna. One out of every eight or ten girls was Annot in Yorkshire at a time when Anna is never found to be in use at all:
"Stephanus Webester, & Anota uxor ejus, iiiid.
"Richard Annotson, wryght, iiiid."—W. D. S.

As Alianora and Eleanora are the same, so were Enot and Anot:
"Henricus filius Johannis Enotson, iiiid."—W. D. S.

Again, Eleanor became Elena, and this Lina and Linot. Hence in the Hundred Rolls we find "Linota atte Field." In fact, the early forms of Eleanor are innumerable. The favourite Sibilla became Sibot:
"Johannes de Estwode, et Sibota uxor ejus, iiiid.
"Willelmus Howeson, et Sibbota uxor ejus, iiiid."—W. D. S.

Mary not merely became Marion, but Mariot, and from our surnames it would appear the latter was the favourite:
"Isabella serviens Mariota Gulle, iiiid."—W. D. S.
"Mariota in le Lane."—Hundred Rolls.

Eve became Evot, Adam and Eve being popular names. In the will of William de Kirkby, dated 1391, are bequests to "Evæ uxori Johannes Parvying" and "Willielmo de Rowlay," and later on he refers to them again as the aforementioned "Evotam et dictum Willielmum Rowlay" ("Test. Ebor.," i. 145. Surtees Society).

But the girl-name that made most mark was originally a boy's name, Theobald. Tibbe was the nick form, and Tibbot the pet name. Very speedily it became the property of the female sex, such entries as Tibot Fitz-piers ending in favour of Tibota Foliot. After the year 1300 Tib, or Tibet, is invariably feminine. In "Gammer Gurton's Needle," Gammer says to her maid—
"How now, Tib? quick! let's hear what news thou hast brought hither."—Act. i. sc. 5.

In "Ralph Roister Doister," the pet name is used in the song, evidently older than the play:
"Pipe, merry Annot, etc.,
Trilla, Trilla, Trillary.
Work, Tibet; work, Annot; work, Margery;
Sew, Tibet; knit, Annot; spin, Margery;
Let us see who will win the victory."

Gib, from Gilbert, and Tib became the common name for a male and female cat. Scarcely any other terms were employed from 1350 to 1550:

"For right no more than Gibbe, our cat,
That awaiteth mice and rattes to killen,
Ne entend I but to beguilen."

Hence both Tibet and Gibbet were also used for the same; as in the old phrase "flitter-gibbett," for one of wanton character. Tom in tom-cat came into ordinary parlance later. All our modern Tibbots, Tibbetts, Tibbitts, Tippitts, Tebbutts, and their endless other forms, are descended from Tibbe.

Coming to boys' names, all our Wyatts in the Directory hail from Guiot, the diminutive of Guy, just as Wilmot from William:

"Adam, son of Wyot, held an oxgang of land."—"De Lacy Inquisition."

"Ibbote Wylymot, iiiid."—W. D. S.

Payn is met in the form of Paynot and Paynet, Warin as Warinot, Drew as Drewet, Philip as Philpot, though this is feminine sometimes:

"Johannes Schikyn, et Philipot uxor ejus, iiiid."—W. D. S.

Thomas is found as Thomaset, Higg (Isaac) as Higgot, Jack as Jackett, Hal (Henry) as Hallet (Harriot or Harriet is now feminine), and Hugh or Hew as Hewet:

"Dionisia Howet-doghter, iiiid."—W. D. S.

The most interesting, perhaps, of these examples is Hamnet, or Hamlet. Hamon, or Hamond, was introduced from Normandy:

"Hamme, son of Adcock, held 29 acres of land."—"De Lacy Inquisition," 1311.

It became a favourite among high and low, and took to itself the forms of Hamonet and Hamelot:

"The wife of Richard, son of Hamelot."—"De Lacy Inquisition," 1311.

These were quickly abbreviated into Hamnet and Hamlet. They ran side by side for several centuries, and at last, like Emmot, defied the English Bible, the Reformation, and even the Puritan period, and lived unto the eighteenth century. Hamlet Winstanley, the painter, was born in 1700, at Warrington, and died in 1756. In Kent's London Directory for 1736 several Hamnets occur as baptismal names. Shakespeare's little son was Hamnet, or Hamlet, after his godfather Hamnet Sadler. I find several instances where both forms are entered as the name of the same boy:

"Nov. 13, 1502. Item: the same day to Hamlet Clegge, for money by him layed out ... to the keper of Dachet Ferrey in rewarde for conveying the Quenes grace over Thamys there, iiis. iiiid."

Compare this with—

"June 13, 1502. Item: the same day to Hampnet Clegge, for mone by him delivered to the Quene for hir offring to Saint Edward at Westm., vis. viiid."—"Privy Purse Expenses, Eliz. of York," pp. 21 and 62.

Speaking of Hamelot, we must not forget that ot and et sometimes became elot or elet. As a diminutive it is found in such dictionary words as bracelet, tartlet, gimblet, poplet (for poppet). The old ruff or high collar worn alike by men and women was styled a partlet:

"Jan. 1544. Item: from Mr. Braye ii. high collar partletts, iiis. ixd."—"Privy Purse Expenses,

Princess Mary."

Hence partlet, a hen, on account of the ruffled feathers, a term used alike by Chaucer and Shakespeare.

In our nomenclature we have but few traces of it. In France it was very commonly used. But Hughelot or Huelot, from Hugh, was popular, as our Hewletts can testify. Richelot for Richard, Hobelot and Robelot for Robert, Crestolot for Christopher, Cesselot for Cecilia, and Barbelot for Barbara, are found also, and prove that the desinence had made its mark.

Returning, however, to ot and et: Eliot or Elliot, from Ellis (Elias), had a great run. In the north it is sometimes found as Aliot:

"Alyott de Symondeston held half an oxgang of land, xixd."—"De Lacy Inquisition," 1311.

The feminine form was Elisot or Elicot, although this was used also for boys. The will of William de Aldeburgh, written in 1319, runs—

"Item: do et lego Elisotæ domicellæ meæ 40s."—"Test. Ebor.," i. 151.

The will of Patrick de Barton, administered in the same year, says—

"Item: lego Elisotæ, uxori Ricardi Bustard unam vaccam, et 10s."—"Test. Ebor.," i. 155.

"Eliseus Carpenter, cartwyth, et Elesot uxor ejus, vid."—W. D. S.

As Ellis became Ellisot, so Ellice became Ellicot, whence the present surname. Bartholomew became Bartelot, now Bartlett, and from the pet form Toll, or Tolly, came Tollett and Tollitt.

It is curious to notice why Emmot and Hamlet, or Hamnet, survived the crises that overwhelmed the others. Both became baptismal names in their own right. People forgot in course of time that they were diminutives of Emma and Hamond, and separated them from their parents. This did not come about till the close of Elizabeth's reign, so they have still the credit of having won a victory against terrible odds, the Hebrew army. Hamnet Shakespeare was so baptized. Hamon or Hamond would have been the regular form.

Looking back, it is hard to realize that a custom equally affected by prince and peasant, as popular in country as town, as familiar in Yorkshire and Lancashire as in London and Winchester, should have been so completely uprooted, that ninety-nine out of the hundred are now unaware that it ever existed. This was unmistakably the result of some disturbing element of English social life. At the commencement of the sixteenth century there was no appearance of this confusion. In France the practice went on without let or hindrance. We can again but attribute it to the Reformation, and the English Bible, which swept away a large batch of the old names, and pronounced the new without addition or diminution. When some of the old names were restored, it was too late to fall back upon the familiarities that had been taken with them in the earlier period.

(e.) Double Terminatives.

In spite of the enormous popularity in England of ot and et, they bear no proportion to the number in France. In England our local surnames are two-fifths of the whole. In France patronymic surnames are almost two-fifths of the whole. Terminatives in on or in, and ot and et, have done this. We in England only adopted double diminutives in two cases, those of Colinet and Robinet, or Dobinet, and both were rarely used. Robinet has come down to us as a surname;

and Dobinet so existed till the middle of the fifteenth century, for one John Dobynette is mentioned in an inventory of goods, 1463 (Mun. Acad. Oxon.). This Dobinet seems to have been somewhat familiarly used, for Dobinet Doughty is Ralph's servant in "Ralph Roister Doister." Matthew Merrygreek says—

"I know where she is: Dobinet hath wrought some wile.

Tibet Talkapace. He brought a ring and token, which he said was sent

From our dame's husband."—Act. iii. sc. 2.

Colin is turned into Colinet in Spenser's "Shepherd's Calendar," where Colin beseeches Pan:

"Hearken awhile from thy green cabinet,

The laurel song of careful Colinet?"

Jannet is found as Janniting (Jannetin) once on English soil, for in the "London Chanticleers," a comedy written about 1636, Janniting is the apple-wench. Welcome says—

"Who are they which they're enamoured so with?

Bung. The one's Nancy Curds, and the other Hanna Jenniting: Ditty and Jenniting are agreed already ... the wedding will be kept at our house."—Scene xiii.

But the use of double diminutives was of every-day practice in Normandy and France, and increased their total greatly. I take at random the following surnames (originally, of course, christian names) from the Paris Directory:—Margotin, Marioton, Lambinet (Lambert), Perrinot, Perrotin, Philiponet, Jannotin, Hugonet, Huguenin, Jacquinot, and Fauconnet (English Fulke). Huguenin (little wee Hugh) repeats the same diminutive; Perrinot and Perrotin (little wee Peter) simply reverse the order of the two diminutives. The "marionettes" in the puppet-show take the same liberty with Mariotin (little wee Mary) above mentioned. Hugonet, of course, is the same as Huguenot; and had English, not to say French, writers remembered this old custom, they would have found no difficulty in reducing the origin of the religious sect of that name to an individual as a starting-point. Guillotin (little wee William) belongs to the same class, and descended from a baptismal name to become the surname of the famous doctor who invented the deadly machine that bears his title. I have discovered one instance of this as a baptismal name, viz. Gillotyne Hansake ("Wars of English in France: Henry VI.," vol. ii. p. 531).

Returning to England, we find these pet forms in use well up to the Reformation:

"Nov., 1543. Item: geven to Fylpot, my Lady of Suffolk's lackaye, viis. vid.

"June, 1537. Item: payed to Typkyn for cherys, xxd."—"Privy Purse Expenses, Princess Mary."

"1548, July 22. Alson, d. of Jenkin Rowse."—St. Columb Major.

"1545, Oct. 3. Baptized Alison, d. of John James."—Ditto.

"Ralph Roister Doister," written not earlier than 1545, and not later than 1550, by Nicholas Udall, contains three characters styled Annot Alyface, Tibet Talkapace, and Dobinet Doughty. Christian Custance, Sim Suresby, Madge Mumblecheek, and Gawyn Goodluck are other characters, all well-known contemporary names.

In "Thersites," an interlude written in 1537, there is mention of

"Simkin Sydnam, Sumnor,

That killed a cat at Cumnor."

Jenkin Jacon is introduced, also Robin Rover. In a book entitled "Letters and Papers, Foreign and Domestic" (Henry VIII.), we find a document (numbered 1939, and dated 1526) containing a list of the household attendants and retinue of the king. Even here, although so formal a record, there occurs the name of "Hamynet Harrington, gentleman usher."

We may assert with the utmost certainty that, on the eve of the Hebrew invasion, there was not a baptismal name in England of average popularity that had not attached to it in daily converse one or other of these diminutives—kin, cock, in, on, ot, and et; not a name, too, that, before it had thus attached them, had not been shorn of all its fulness, and curtailed to a monosyllabic nick form. Bartholomew must first become Bat before it becomes Batcock, Peter must become Pierre before Perrot can be formed, Nicholas must be abbreviated to Col or Cole before Col or Cole can be styled Colin, and Thomas must be reduced to Tom before Tomkin can make his appearance.

Several names had attached to themselves all these enclytics. For instance, Peter is met with, up to the crisis we are about to consider, in the several shapes of Perkin or Parkin, Peacock, Perrot, and Perrin; and William as Willin (now Willing and Willan in our directories), Wilcock, Wilkin, and Wilmot, was familiar to every district in the country.

III. Scripture Names already in use at the Reformation.

It now remains simply to consider the state of nomenclature in England at the eve of the Reformation in relation to the Bible. Four classes may be mentioned.

(a.) Mystery Names.

The leading incidents of Bible narrative were familiarized to the English lower orders by the performance of sacred plays, or mysteries, rendered under the supervision of the Church. To these plays we owe the early popularity of Adam and Eve, Noah, Abraham, Isaac, Jacob, Joseph, Sara, Daniel, Sampson, Susanna, Judith, Hanna or Anna, and Hester. But the Apocryphal names were not frequently used till about 1500. Scarcely any diminutives are found of them. On the other hand, Adam became Adcock and Adkin; Eve, Evott and Evett; Isaac, Hickin, and Higgin, and Higgot, and Higget; Joseph, Joskin; and Daniel, Dankin and Dannet.

(b.) Crusade Names.

The Crusaders gave us several prominent names. To them we are indebted for Baptist, Ellis, and Jordan: and John received a great stimulus. The sacred water brought in the leathern bottle was used for baptismal purposes. The Jordan commemorated John the Baptist, the second Elias, the forerunner and baptizer of Jesus Christ. Children were styled by these incidents. Jordan became popular through Western Europe. In England he gave us, as already observed, Judd, Judkin, Judson, Jordan, and Jordanson. Elias, as Ellis, took about the eighth place of frequency, and John, for a while, the first.

(c.) The Saints' Calendar.

The legends of the saints were carefully taught by the priesthood, and the day as religiously observed. All children born on these holy days received the name of the saint commemorated: St. James's Day, or St. Nicholas's Day, or St. Thomas's Day, saw a small batch of Jameses, Nicholases, and Thomases received into the fold of the Church. In other cases the gossip had some favourite saint, and placed the child under his or her protection. Of course, it bore the patron's name. A large number of these hagiological names were extra-Biblical—such as Cecilia, Catharine, or Theobald. Of these I make no mention here. All the Apostles, save Judas, became household names, John, Simon, Peter, Bartholomew, Matthew, James, Thomas, and Philip being the favourites. Paul and Timothy were also utilized, the former being always found as Pol.

(d.) Festival Names.

If a child was born at Whitsuntide or Easter, Christmas or Epiphany, like Robinson Crusoe's man Friday, or Thursday October Christian of the Pitcairn islanders, he received the name of the day. Hence our once familiar names of Noel or Nowell, Pask or Pascal, Easter, Pentecost, and Epiphany or Tiffany.

It will be observed that all these imply no direct or personal acquaintance with the Scriptures. All came through the Church. All, too, were in the full tide of prosperity—with the single exception of Jordan, which was nearly obsolete—when the Bible, printed into English and set up in our churches, became an institution. The immediate result was that the old Scripture names of Bartholomew, Peter, Philip, and Nicholas received a blow much deadlier than that received by such Teutonic names as Robert, Richard, Roger, and Ralph. But that will be brought out as we progress.

The subject of the influence of an English Bible upon English nomenclature is not uninteresting. It may be said of the "Vulgar Tongue" Bible that it revolutionized our nomenclature within the space of forty years, or little over a generation. No such crisis, surely, ever visited a nation's register before, nor can such possibly happen again. Every home felt the effect. It was like the massacre of the innocents in Egyptian days: "There was not one house where there was not one dead." But in Pharoah's day they did not replace the dead with the living. At the Reformation such a locust army of new names burst upon the land that we may well style it the Hebrew Invasion.

CHAPTER I.

THE HEBREW INVASION.

"With what face can they object to the king the bringing in of forraigners, when themselves entertaine such an army of Hebrewes?" The Character of a London Diurnall (Dec. 1644).

"Albeit in our late Reformation some of good consideration have brought in Zachary, Malachy, Josias, etc., as better agreeing with our faith, but without contempt of Country names (as I hope) which have both good and gracious significations, as shall appeare hereafter."—Camden, Remaines. 1614.

I. The March of the Army.

The strongest impress of the English Reformation to-day is to be seen in our font-names. The majority date from 1560, the year when the Genevan Bible was published. This version ran through unnumbered editions, and for sixty, if not seventy, years was the household Bible of the nation. The Genevan Bible was not only written in the vulgar tongue, but was printed for vulgar hands. A moderate quarto was its size; all preceding versions, such as Coverdale's, Matthew's, and of course the Great Bible, being the ponderous folio, specimens of which the reader will at some time or other have seen. The Genevan Bible, too, was the Puritan's Bible, and was none the less admired by him on account of its Calvinistic annotations.

But although the rage for Bible names dates from the decade 1560-1570, which decade marks the rise of Puritanism, there had been symptoms of the coming revolution as early as 1543. Richard Hilles, one of the Reformers, despatching a letter from Strasburg, November 15, 1543, writes:

"My wife says she has no doubt but that God helped her the sooner in her confinement by reason of your good prayers. On the second of this month she brought forth to the Church of Christ a son, who, as the women say, is quite large enough for a mother of tall stature, and whom I immediately named Gershom."—"Original Letters," 1537-1558, No. cxii. Parker Society.

We take up our Bibles, and find that of Zipporah it is said—

"And she bare him (Moses) a son, and he called his name Gershom: for he said, I have been a stranger in a strange land."—Exod. ii. 22.

The margin says, "a desolate stranger." At this time Moses was fled from Pharaoh, who would kill him. The parallel to Richard Hilles's mind was complete. This was in 1643.

In Mr. Tennyson's drama "Mary," we have the following scene between Gardiner and a yokel:

"Gardiner.I distrust thee,

There is a half voice, and a lean assent:

What is thy name?

Man.Sanders!

Gardiner.What else?

Man.Zerrubabel."

The Laureate was right to select for this rebellious Protestant a name that was to be popular throughout Elizabeth's reign; but poetic license runs rather far in giving this title to a full-grown man in any year of Mary's rule. Sanders might have had a young child at home so styled, but for himself it was practically impossible. So clearly defined is the epoch that saw, if not one batch of names go out, at least a new batch come in. Equally marked are the names from the Bible which at this date were in use, and those which were not. Of this latter category Zerrubabel was one.

In the single quotation from Hilles's letter of 1543 we see the origin of the great Hebrew invasion explained. The English Bible had become a fact, and the knowledge of its personages and narratives was becoming directly acquired. In every community up and down the country it was as if a fresh spring of clear water had been found, and every neighbour could come with jug or pail, and fill it when and how they would. One of the first impressions made seems to have been this: children in the olden time received as a name a term that was immediately significant of the circumstances of their birth. Often God personally, through His prophets or angelic messenger, acted as godparent indeed, and gave the name, as in Isaiah viii. 1, 3, 4:

"Moreover the Lord said unto me, Take thee a great roll, and write in it with a man's pen concerning Maher-shalal-hash-baz.

"And I went unto the prophetess; and she conceived, and bare a son. Then said the Lord to me, Call his name Maher-shalal-hash-baz.

"For before the child shall have knowledge to cry, My father, and my mother, the riches of Damascus and the spoil of Samaria shall be taken away before the king of Assyria."

Here was a name palpably significant. Even before they knew its exact meaning the name was enrolled in English church registers, and by-and-by zealot Puritans employed it as applicable to English Church politics.

All the patriarchs, down to the twelve sons of Jacob, had names of direct significance given them. Above all, a peculiar emphasis was laid upon all the titles of Jesus Christ, as in Isaiah vii. 14:

"Behold, a virgin shall conceive, and bear a son, and shall call his name Immanuel."

At the same time that this new revelation came, a crisis was going on of religion. The old Romish Church was being uprooted, or, rather, a new system was being grafted upon its stock, for the links have never been broken. The saints were shortly to be tabooed by the large mass of English folk; the festivals were already at a discount. Simultaneously with the prejudice against the very names of their saints and saintly festivals, arose the discovery of a mine of new names as novel as it was unexhaustible. They not merely met the new religious instinct, but supplied what would have been a very serious vacuum.

But we must at once draw a line between the Reformation and Puritanism. Previous to the Reformation, so far as the Church was concerned, there had been to a certain extent a system of nomenclature. The Reformation abrogated that system, but did not intentionally adopt a new one. Puritanism deliberately supplied a well-weighed and revised scheme, beyond which no adopted child of God must dare to trespass. Previous to the Reformation, the priest, with the assent of the gossip, gave the babe the name of the saint who was to be its patron, or on whose day the birth or baptism occurred. If the saint was a male, and the infant a female, the difficulty was overcome by giving the name a feminine form. Thus Theobald become Theobalda; and hence Tib and Tibot became so common among girls, that finally they ceased to represent boys at all. If it were one of the great holy days, the day or season itself furnished the name. Thus it was Simon, or Nicholas, or Cecilia, or Austen, or Pentecost, or Ursula, or Dorothy, became so familiar. From the reign of Elizabeth the clergy, and Englishmen generally, gave up this practice. Saints who could not boast apostolic honours were rejected, and holy men of lesser prestige, together with a large batch of virgins and martyrs of the Agnes, Catharine, and Ursula type, who belonged to Church history, received but scant attention. As a matter of course their names lapsed. But the nation stood by the old English names not thus popishly tainted. Against Geoffrey, Richard, Robert, and William, they had no prejudice: nay, they clung to them. The Puritan rejected both classes. He was ever trotting out his two big "P's,"—Pagan and Popish. Under the first he placed every name that could not be found in the Scriptures, and under the latter every title in the same Scriptures, and the Church system founded on them, that had been employed previous, say, to the coronation day of Edward VI. Of this there is the clearest proof. In a "Directory of Church Government," found among the papers of Cartwright, and written as early as 1565, there is the following order regarding and regulating baptism:—

"They which present unto baptism, ought to be persuaded not to give those that are baptized the names of God, or of Christ, or of angels, or of holy offices, as of baptist, evangelist, etc., nor such as savour of paganism or popery: but chiefly such whereof there are examples, in the Holy Scriptures, in the names of those who are reported in them to have been godly and virtuous."—Neale, vol. v. Appendix, p. 15.

Nothing can be more precise than this. To the strict Puritan to reject the Richards, Mileses, and Henrys of the Teutonic, and the Bartholomews, Simons, Peters, and Nicholases of the ecclesiastic class, was to remove the Canaanite out of the land.

How early this "article of religion" was obeyed, one or two quotations will show. Take the first four baptismal entries in the Canterbury Cathedral register:

"1564, Dec. 3. Abdias, the sonne of Robert Pownoll.
"1567, April 26. Barnabas, the sonne of Robert Pownoll.
"1569, June 1. Ezeckiell, the sonne of Robert Pownoll.
"1572, Feb. 10. Posthumus, the sonne of Robert Pownoll."

Another son seems to have been Philemon:

"1623, April 27. John, the sonne of Philemon Pownoll."

A daughter "Repentance" must be added:

"1583, Dec. 8. Married William Arnolde and Repentance Pownoll."

Take another instance, a little later, from the baptisms of St. Peter's, Cornhill:

"1589, Nov. 2. Bezaleell, sonne of Michaell Nichollson, cordwayner.
"1599, Sep. 23. Aholiab, sonne of Michaell Nicholson, cordwainer.
"1595, May 18. Sara, daughter of Michaell Nichollson, cobler.
"1599, Nov. 1. Buried Rebecca, daughter of Michaell Nicholson, cordwainer, 13 yeares."

Rebecca, therefore, would be baptized in 1586. Sara and Aholiab died of the plague in 1603. Both old Robert Pownoll and the cobler must have been Puritans of a pronounced type.

The Presbyterian clergy were careful to set an example of right name-giving:

"1613, July 28. Baptized Jaell, daughter of Roger Mainwaring, preacher."—St. Helen, Bishopsgate.

"1617, Jan. 25. Baptized Ezekyell, sonne of Mr. Richard Culverwell, minister."—St. Peter, Cornhill.

"1582, ——. Buried Zachary, sonne of Thomas Newton, minister."—Barking, Essex.

A still more interesting proof comes from Northampton. As an example of bigotry it is truly marvellous. On July 16, 1590, Archbishop Whitgift furnished the Lord Treasurer with the following, amongst many articles against Edmond Snape, curate of St. Peter's, in that town:

"Item: Christopher Hodgekinson obteyned a promise of the said Snape that he would baptize his child; but Snape added, saying, 'You must then give it a christian name allowed in the Scriptures.' Then Hodgekinson told him that his wife's father, whose name was Richard, desired to have the giving of that name."

At the time of service Snape proceeded till they came to the place of naming: they said "Richard;"

"But hearing them calling it Richard, and that they would not give it any other name, he stayed there, and would not in any case baptize the child. And so it was carried away thence, and was baptized the week following at Allhallows Churche, and called Richard."—Strype's "Whitgift," ii. 9.

This may be an extreme case, but I doubt not the majority of the Presbyterian clergy did their best to uproot the old English names, so far as their power of persuasion could go.

Even the pulpit was used in behalf of the new doctrine. William Jenkin, the afterwards ejected minister, in his "Expositions of Jude," delivered in Christ Church, London, said, while commenting on the first verse, "Our baptismal names ought to be such as may prove remembrances of duty." He then instances Leah, Alpheus, and Hannah as aware of parental obligations in this respect, and adds—

"'Tis good to impose such names as expresse our baptismal promise. A good name is as a thread tyed about the finger, to make us mindful of the errand we came into the world to do for our Master."—Edition 1652, p. 7.

As a general rule, the New Testament names spread the most rapidly, especially girl-names of the Priscilla, Dorcas, Tabitha, and Martha type. They were the property of the Reformation. Damaris bothered the clerks much, and is found indifferently as Tamaris, Damris, Dammeris, Dampris, and Dameris. By James I.'s day it had become a fashionable name:

"1617, April 13. Christened Damaris, d. of Doctor Masters.

"——, May 29. Christened Damaris, d. of Doctor Kingsley."—Canterbury Cathedral.

Martha, which sprang into instant popularity, is registered at the outset:

"1563, July 25. Christened Martha Wattam."—St. Peter, Cornhill.

Phebe had a great run. The first I have seen is—

"1568, Oct. 24. Christened Phebe, d. of Harry Cut."—St. Peter, Cornhill.

Dorcas was, perhaps, the prime favourite, often styled and entered Darcas. Every register has it, and every page. A political ballad says—

"Come, Dorcas and Cloe,
With Lois and Zoe,
Young Lettice, and Beterice, and Jane;
Phill, Dorothy, Maud,
Come troop it abroad,
For now is our time to reign."

Persis, Tryphena, and Tryphosa were also largely used. The earliest Persis I know is—

"1579, Maye 3. Christened Persis, d. of William Hopkinson, minister heare."—Salehurst.

Some of these names—as, for instance, Priscilla, Damaris, Dorcas, and Phebe—stood in James's reign almost at the head of girls' names in England. Indeed, alike in London and the provinces, the list of girl-names at Elizabeth's death was a perfect contrast to that when she ascended the throne. Then the great national names of Isabella, Matilda, Emma, and Cecilia ruled supreme. Then the four heroines Anna, Judith, Susan, and Hester, one or two of whom were in the Apocryphal narrative, had stamped themselves on our registers in what appeared indelible lines, although they were of much more recent popularity than the others. They lost prestige, but did not die out. Many Puritans had a sneaking fondness for them, finding in their histories a parallel to their own troubles, and perchance they had a private and more godly rendering of the popular ballad of their day:

"In Ninivie old Toby dwelt,
An aged man, and blind was he:
And much affliction he had felt,
Which brought him unto poverty:
He had by Anna, his true wife,
One only sonne, and eke no more."

Esther is still popular in our villages, so is Susan. Hannah has her admirers, and only Judith may be said to be forgotten. But their glory was from 1450 to 1550. After that they became secondary personages. Throughout the south of England, especially in the counties that surrounded London, the Bible had been ransacked from nook to corner. The zealots early dived into the innermost recesses of Scripture. They made themselves as familiar with chapters devoted solely to genealogical tables, as to those which they quoted to defend their doctrinal creed. The eighth chapter of Romans was not more studied by them than the thirty-sixth of Genesis, and the dukes of Edom classified in the one were laid under frequent contribution to witness to the adoption treated of in the other. Thus names unheard of in 1558 were "household words" in 1603.

The slowest to take up the new custom were the northern counties. They were out of the current; and Lancashire, besides being inaccessible, had stuck to the old faith. Names lingered on in the Palatinate that had been dead nearly a hundred years in the south. Gawin figures in all northern registers till a century ago, and Thurston was yet popular in the Fylde district, when it had become forgotten in the Fens. Scotland was never touched at all. The General Assembly of

1645 makes no hint on the subject, although it dwelt on nearly every other topic. Nothing demonstrates the clannish feeling of North Britain as this does. At this moment Scotland has scarcely any Bible names.

In Yorkshire, however, Puritanism made early stand, though its effects on nomenclature were not immediately visible. It was like the fire that smoulders among the underwood before it catches flame; it spreads the more rapidly afterwards. The Genevan Bible crept into the dales and farmsteads, and their own primitive life seemed to be but reflected in its pages. The patriarchs lived as graziers, and so did they. There was a good deal about sheep and kine in its chapters, and their own lives were spent among the milk-pails and wool shears. The women of the Old Testament baked cakes, and knew what good butter was. So did the dales' folk. By slow degrees Cecilia, Isabella, and Emma lapsed from their pedestal, and the little babes were turned into Sarahs, Rebeccas, and Deborahs. As the seventeenth century progressed the state of things became still more changed. There had been villages in Sussex and Kent previous to Elizabeth's death, where the Presbyterian rector, by his personal influence at the time of baptism, had turned the new generation into a Hebrew colony. The same thing occurred in Yorkshire only half a century later. As nonconformity gained ground, Guy, and Miles, and Peter, and Philip became forgotten. The lads were no sooner ushered into existence than they were transformed into duplicates of Joel, and Amos, and Obediah. The measles still ran through the family, but it was Phineas and Caleb, not Robert and Roger, that underwent the infliction. Chosen leaders of Israel passed through the critical stages of teething. As for the twelve sons of Jacob, they could all have answered to their names in the dames' schools, through their little apple-cheeked representatives, who lined the rude benches. On the village green, every prophet from Isaiah to Malachi might be seen of an evening playing leap-frog: unless, indeed, Zephaniah was stealing apples in the garth.

From Yorkshire, about the close of the seventeenth century, the rage for Scripture names passed into Lancashire. Nonconformity was making progress; the new industries were already turning villages into small centres of population, and the Church of England not providing for the increase, chapels were built. If we look over the pages of the directories of West Yorkshire and East Lancashire, and strike out the surnames, we could imagine we were consulting anciently inscribed registers of Joppa or Jericho. It would seem as if Canaan and the West Riding had got inextricably mixed.

What a spectacle meets our eye! Within the limits of ten leaves we have three Pharoahs, while as many Hephzibahs are to be found on one single page. Adah and Zillah Pickles, sisters, are milliners. Jehoiada Rhodes makes saws—not Solomon's sort—and Hariph Crawshaw keeps a farm. Vashni, from somewhere in the Chronicles, is rescued from oblivion by Vashni Wilkinson, coal merchant, who very likely goes to Barzillai Williamson, on the same page, for his joints, Barzillai being a butcher. Jachin, known to but a few as situated in the Book of Kings, is in the person of Jachin Firth, a beer retailer, familiar to all his neighbours. Heber Holdsworth on one page is faced by Er Illingworth on the other. Asa and Joab are extremely popular, while Abner, Adna, Ashael, Erastus, Eunice, Benaiah, Aquila, Elihu, and Philemon enjoy a fair amount of patronage. Shadrach, Meshach, and Abednego, having been rescued from Chaldæan fire, have been deluged with baptismal water. How curious it is to contemplate such entries as Lemuel Wilson, Kelita Wilkinson, Shelah Haggas, Shadrach Newbold, Neriah Pearce, Jeduthan Jempson, Azariah Griffiths, Naphtali Matson, Philemon Jakes, Hameth Fell, Eleph Bisat, Malachi Ford, or Shallum Richardson. As to other parts of the Scriptures, I have lighted upon name after name that I did not know existed in the Bible at all till I looked into the Lancashire and Yorkshire directories.

The Bible has decided the nomenclature of the north of England. In towns like Oldham, Bolton, Ashton, and Blackburn, the clergyman's baptismal register is but a record of Bible names. A clerical friend of mine christened twins Cain and Abel, only the other day, much against his own wishes. Another parson on the Derbyshire border was gravely informed, at the proper moment, that the name of baptism was Ramoth-Gilead. "Boy or girl, eh?" he asked in a somewhat agitated voice. The parents had opened the Bible hap-hazard, according to the village tradition, and selected the first name the eye fell on. It was but a year ago a little child was christened Tellno in a town within six miles of Manchester, at the suggestion of a cotton-spinner, the father, a workman of the name of Lees, having asked his advice. "I suppose it must be a Scripture name," said his master. "Oh yes! that's of course." "Suppose you choose Tellno," said his employer. "That'll do," replied the other, who had never heard it before, and liked it the better on that account. The child is now Tell-no Lees, the father, too late, finding that he had been hoaxed. "Sirs," was the answer given to a bewildered curate, after the usual demand to name the child. He objected, but was informed that it was a Scripture name, and the verse "Sirs, what must I do to be saved?" was triumphantly appealed to. This reminds one of the Puritan who styled his dog "Moreover" after the dog in the Gospel: "Moreover the dog came and licked his sores."

There is, again, a story of a clergyman making the customary demand as to name from a knot of women round the font. "Ax her," said one. Turning to the woman who appeared to be indicated, he again asked, "What name?" "Ax her," she replied. The third woman, being questioned, gave the same reply. At last he discovered the name to be the Scriptural Achsah, Caleb's daughter—a name, by the way, which was somewhat popular with our forefathers. No wonder this mistake arose, when Achsah used to be entered in some such manner as this:

"1743-4, Jan. 3. Baptized Axar Starrs (a woman of ripe years), of Stockport.

"1743-4, Jan. 3. Married Warren Davenport, of Stockport, Esq., and Axar Starrs, aforesaid, spinster."—Marple, Cheshire.

Axar's father was Caleb Starrs. The scriptural relationship was thus preserved. Achsah crossed the Atlantic with the Pilgrim Fathers, and has prospered there ever since. It is still popular in Devonshire and the south-west of England. All these stories serve to show the quarry whence modern names are hewn.

I have mentioned the north because I have studied its Post-Office Directories carefully. But if any one will visit the shires of Dorset, and Devon, and Hampshire, he will find the same result. The Hebrew has won the day. Just as in England, north of Trent, we can still measure off the ravages of the Dane by striking a line through all local names lying westward ending in "by," so we have but to count up the baptismal names of the peasantry of these southern counties to see that they have become the bondsmen of an Eastern despot. In fact, go where and when we will from the reign of Elizabeth, we find the same influence at work. Take a few places and people at random.

Looking at our testamentary records, we find the will of Kerenhappuch Benett proved in 1762, while Kerenhappuch Horrocks figures in the Manchester Directory for 1877. Onesiphorus Luffe appears on a halfpenny token of 1666; Habakkuk Leyman, 1650; Euodias Inman, 1650; Melchisedek Fritter, 1650; Elnathan Brock, 1654; and Abdiah Martin, 1664 ("Tokens of Seventeenth Century"). Shallum Stent was married in 1681 (Racton, Sussex); Gershom Baylie was constable of Lewes in 1619, Araunah Verrall fulfilling the same office in 1784. Captain Epenetus Crosse presented a petition to Privy Council in 1660 (C. S. P. Colonial); Erastus Johnson was defendant in 1724, and Cressens Boote twenty years earlier. Barjonah Dove was Vicar of Croxton in 1694. Tryphena Monger was buried in Putney Churchyard in 1702, and Tryphosa Saunders at St. Peter's, Worcester, in 1770. Mahaliel Payne, Azarias Phesant, and Pelatiah Barnard are recorded in State Papers, 1650-1663 (C. S. P.), and Aminadab Henley was dwelling in Kent in 1640 ("Proceedings in Kent." Camden Society). Shadrack Pride is a collector of hearth-money in 1699, and Gamaliel Chase is communicated with in 1635 (C. S. P.). Onesiphorus Albin proposes a better plan of collecting the alien duty in 1692 (C. S. P.), while Mordecai Abbott is appointed deputy-paymaster of the forces in 1697 (C. S. P.). Eliakim Palmer is married at Somerset House Chapel in 1740; Dalilah White is buried at Cowley in 1791, and Keziah Simmons is christened there in 1850. Selah Collins is baptized at Dyrham, Gloucestershire, in 1752, and Keturah Jones is interred at Clifton in 1778. Eli-lama-Sabachthani Pressnail was existing in 1862 (Notes and Queries), and the Times recorded a Talitha-Cumi People about the same time. The will of Mahershalalhashbaz Christmas was proved not very long ago. Mrs. Mahershalalhashbaz Bradford was dwelling in Ringwood, Hampshire, in 1863; and on January 31, 1802, the register of Beccles Church received the entry, "Mahershalalhashbaz, son of Henry and Sarah Clarke, baptized," the same being followed, October 14, 1804, by the baptismal entry of "Zaphnaphpaaneah," another son of the same couple. A grant of administration in the estate of Acts-Apostles Pegden was made in 1865. His four brothers, older than himself, were of course the four Evangelists, and had there been a sixth I dare say his name would have been "Romans." An older member of this family, many years one of the kennel-keepers of Tickham fox-hounds, was Pontius Pilate Pegden. At a confirmation at Faversham in 1847, the incumbent of Dunkirk presented to the amazed archbishop a boy named "Acts-Apostles." These are, of course, mere eccentricities, but eccentricities follow a beaten path, and have their use in calculations of the nature we are considering. Eccentricities in dress are proverbially but exaggerations of the prevailing fashion.

II. POPULARITY OF THE OLD TESTAMENT.

The affection felt by the Puritans for the Old Testament has been observed by all writers upon the period, and of the period. Cleveland's remark, quoted by Hume, is, of course, an exaggeration.

"Cromwell," he says, "hath beat up his drums cleane through the Old Testament—you may learne the genealogy of our Saviour by the names in his regiment. The muster-master uses no other list than the first chapter of Matthew."

Lord Macaulay puts it much more faithfully in his first chapter, speaking, too, of an earlier period than the Commonwealth:

"In such a history (i.e. Old Testament) it was not difficult for fierce and gloomy spirits to find much that might be distorted to suit their wishes. The extreme Puritans, therefore, began to feel for the Old Testament a preference which, perhaps, they did not distinctly avow even to themselves, but which showed itself in all their sentiments and habits. They paid to the Hebrew language a respect which they refused to that tongue in which the discourses of Jesus and the Epistles of Paul have come down to us. They baptized their children by the names, not of Christian saints, but of Hebrew patriarchs and warriors."

The Presbyterian clergy had another objection to the New Testament names. The possessors were all saints, and in the saints' calendar. The apostolic title was as a red rag to his blood-shot eye.

"Upon Saint Peter, Paul, John, Jude, and James,

They will not put the 'saint' unto their names,"

says the Water-poet in execrable verse. Its local use was still more trying, as no man could pass through a single quarter of London without seeing half a dozen churches, or lanes, or taverns dedicated to Saint somebody or other.

"Others to make all things recant

The christian and surname of saint,

Would force all churches, streets, and towns

The holy title to renounce."

To avoid any saintly taint, the Puritan avoided the saints themselves.

But the discontented party in the Church had, as Macaulay says, a decided hankering after the Old Testament on other grounds than this. They paid the Hebrew language an almost superstitious reverence. Ananias, the deacon, in the "Alchemist," published in 1610, says—

"Heathen Greek, I take it.

Subtle. How! heathen Greek?

Ananias. All's heathen but the Hebrew."

Bishop Corbet, in his "Distracted Puritan," has a lance to point at the same weakness:

"In the holy tongue of Canaan

I placed my chiefest pleasure,

Till I pricked my foot

With an Hebrew root,

That I bled beyond all measure."

In the "City Match," written by Mayne in 1639, Bannsright says—

"Mistress Dorcas,

If you'll be usher to that holy, learned woman,

That can heal broken shins, scald heads, and th' itch,
Your schoolmistress: that can expound, and teaches
To knit in Chaldee, and work Hebrew samplers,
I'll help you back again."

The Puritan was ever nicknamed after some Old Testament worthy. I could quote many instances, but let two from the author of the "London Diurnall" suffice. Addressing Prince Rupert, he says—

"Let the zeal-twanging nose, that wants a ridge,
Snuffling devoutly, drop his silver bridge:
Yes, and the gossip's spoon augment the summe,
Altho' poor Caleb lose his christendome."

More racy is his attack on Pembroke, as a member of the Mixed Assembly:

"Forbeare, good Pembroke, be not over-daring:
Such company may chance to spoil thy swearing;
And these drum-major oaths of bulk unruly
May dwindle to a feeble 'by my truly.'
He that the noble Percy's blood inherits,
Will he strike up a Hotspur of the spirits?
He'll fright the Obediahs out of tune,
With his uncircumcis-ed Algernoon:
A name so stubborne, 'tis not to be scanned
By him in Gath with the six fingered hand."

If a Bible quotation was put into the zealot's mouth, his cynical foe took care that it should come from the older Scriptures. In George Chapman's "An Humorous Day's Work," after Lemot has suggested a "full test of experiment" to prove her virtue, Florilla the Puritan cries—

"O husband, this is perfect trial indeed."

To which the gruff Labervele replies—

"And you will try all this now, will you not?

Florilla. Yes, my good head: for it is written, we must pass to perfection through all temptation: Abacuk the fourth.

Labervele. Abacuk! cuck me no cucks: in a-doors, I say: thieves, Puritans, murderers! in a-doors, I say!"

In the same facetious strain, Taylor, the Water-poet, addresses a child thus:

"To learne thy duty reade no more than this:
Paul's nineteenth chapter unto Genesis."

This certainly tallies with the charge in "Hudibras," that they

"Corrupted the Old Testament
To serve the New as precedent."

This affection for the older Scriptures had its effect upon our nomenclature. No book, no story, especially if gloomy in its outline and melancholy in its issues, escaped the more morbid

Puritan's notice. Every minister of the Lord's vengeance, every stern witness against natural abomination, the prophet that prophesied ill—these were the names that were in favour. And he that was least bitter in his maledictions was most at a discount. Shadrach, Meshach, and Abednego were in every-day request, Shadrach and Abednego being the favourites. Mordecai, too, was daily commemorated; while Jeremiah attained a popularity, as Jeremy, he can never altogether lose. "Lamentations" was so melancholy, that it must needs be personified, don a Puritanical habit, and stand at the font as godfather—I mean witness—to some wretched infant who had done nothing to merit such a fate. "Lamentations Chapman" appeared as defendant in a suit in Chancery about 1590. The exact date is not to be found, but the case was tried towards the close of Elizabeth's reign ("Chancery Suits, Elizabeth").

It is really hard to say why names of melancholy import became so common. Perhaps it was a spirit morbidly brooding on the religious oppressions of the times; perhaps it was bile. Any way, Camden says "Dust" and "Ashes" were names in use in the days of Elizabeth and James. These, no doubt, were translations of the Hebrew "Aphrah" into the "vulgar tongue," the name having become exceedingly common. Micah, in one of the most mournful prophecies of the Old Testament, says—

"Declare ye it not at Gath, weep ye not at all: in the house of Aphrah roll thyself in the dust." Literally: "in the house of dust roll thyself in the dust." The name was quickly seized upon:
"Sept., 1599. Baptized Affray, d. of Richard Manne of Lymehus."—Stepney.
"May 15, 1576. Wedding of William Brickhead and Affera Lawrence."—St. Peter's, Cornhill.
This last entry proves how early the name had arisen. In Kent it had become very common. The registers of Canterbury Cathedral teem with it:
"1601, June 5. Christened Afra, the daughter of William Warriner.
"1614, Oct. 30. Christened Aphora, the daughter of Mr. Merrewether.
"1635, July 20. Robert Fuller maryed Apherie Pitt."
In these instances we see at a glance the origin of the licentious Aphra Behn's name, which looks so like a nom-de-plume, and has puzzled many. She was born at Canterbury, with the surname of Johnson, baptized Aphra, and married a Dutch merchant named Behn. When acting as a Government spy at Antwerp in 1666, she signs a letter "Aphara Behn" (C. S. P.), which is nearer the Biblical form than many others. It is just possible her father might have rolled himself several times in the dust had he lived to read some of his daughter's writings. Their tone is not Puritanic. The name has become obsolete; indeed, it scarcely survived the seventeenth century, dying out within a hundred years of its rise. But it was very popular in its day.

Rachel, in her dying pains, had styled, under deep depression, her babe Benoni ("son of my sorrow"); but his father turned it into the more cheerful Benjamin ("son of the right hand"). Of course, Puritanism sided with the mother, and the Benonis flourished at a ratio of six to one over the Benjamins:
"1607. Christened Benony, sonne of Beniamyn Ruthin, mariner."—Stepney.
"1661, Dec. 20. Christened Margrett, d. of Bennoni Wallington, goldsmith."—St. Dionis Backchurch.

"1637, May 6. Order to transmit Benoni Bucke to England from Virginia."—"C. S. P. Colonial."

"1656, March 25. Petition of Benoni Honeywood."—"C. S. P. Colonial."

I don't think, however, all these mothers died in childbed. It would speak badly for the chirurgic skill of the seventeenth century if they did. It was the Church of Christ that was in travail.

Ichabod was equally common. There was something hard and unrelenting in Jael (already mentioned) that naturally suited the temper of every fanatic:

"1613, July 28. Christened Jaell, d. of Roger Manwaryng, preacher."—St. Helen, Bishopsgate.

Mehetabell had something in it, probably its length, that made it popular among the Puritan faction. It lasted well, too:

"1680, March 24. Married Philip Penn and Mehittabela Hilder."—Cant. Cath.

"1693, May 21. Baptized Mehetabell, d. of Jeremiah Hart, apothecary."—St. Dionis Backchurch.

But while Deborah, an especial pet of the fanatics, Sara, Rebecca, Rachel, Zipporah, and Leah were in high favour as Old Testament heroines, none had such a run as Abigail:

"1573, Oct. Abigoll Cumberford, christened."—Stepney.

"1617, Oct. 15. Christened Abbigale, d. of John Webb, shoemaker."—St. Peter, Cornhill.

"1635, Jan. 19. Married Jarrett Birkhead and Abigaile Whitehead."—Ditto.

"May 30, 1721. Married Robert Elles and Abigail Six."—Cant. Cath.

Few Scripture names made themselves so popular as this. At the conclusion of the sixteenth century it was beginning its career, and by Queen Anne's day had reached its zenith. When the Cavalier was drinking at the alehouse, he would waggishly chant through his nose, with eye upturned—

"Come, sisters, and sing
An hymne to our king,
Who sitteth on high degree.
The men at Whitehall,
And the wicked, shall fall,
And hey, then, up go we!
'A match,' quoth my sister Joice,
'Contented,' quoth Rachel, too;
Quoth Abigaile, 'Yea,' and Faith, 'Verily,'
And Charity, 'Let it be so.'"

A curious error has been propagated by writers who ought to have known better. It is customarily asserted that abigail, as a cant term for a waiting-maid, only arose after Abigail Hill, the Duchess of Marlborough's cousin, became waiting-woman to the queen, and supplanted her kinswoman. Certainly we find both Swift and Fielding using the term after this event. But there is good reason for believing that the sobriquet is as old as Charles I.'s reign. Indeed, there can be no reasonable doubt but that we owe the term to the enormous popularity of Beaumont's comedy, "The Scornful Ladie," written about 1613, and played in 1616. The chief part falls to the lot of "Abigal, a waiting-gentlewoman," as the dramatis personæ styles her, the playwright associating the name and employment after the scriptural narrative. But Beaumont knew his Bible well.

That Abigail at once became a cant term is proved by "The Parson's Wedding," written by Killigrew some time between 1645 and 1650. Wanton addresses the Parson:

"Was she deaf to your report?

Parson. Yes, yes.

Wanton. And Ugly, her abigail, she had her say, too?

Parson. Yes, yes."

That this sentence would never have been written but for Beaumont's play, there can be no reasonable doubt. It was performed so late as 1783. In 1673, after yearly performances, it was published as a droll, and entitled "The False Heir." In 1742 it appears again under the title of "The Feigned Shipwreck." Samuel Pepys, in his Diary, records his visits to the playhouse to see "The Scornful Lady" at least four times, viz. 1661, 1662, 1665, and 1667. Writing December 27, 1665, he says—

"By coach to the King's Playhouse, and there saw 'The Scornful Lady' well acted: Doll Common doing Abigail most excellently."

Abigail passed out of favour about the middle of the last century, but Mrs. Masham's artifices had little to do with it. The comedy had done its work, and Abigail coming into use, like Malkin two centuries before, as the cant term for a kitchen drab, or common serving wench, as is sufficiently proved by the literature of the day, the name lost caste with all classes, and was compelled to bid adieu to public favour.

This affection for the Old Testament has never died out among the Nonconformists. The large batch of names I have already quoted from modern directories is almost wholly from the earlier Testament. Wherever Dissent is strong, there will be found a large proportion of these names. Amongst the passengers who went out to New England in James and Charles's reigns will be found such names as Ebed-meleck Gastrell, Oziell Lane, Ephraim Howe, Ezechell Clement, Jeremy Clement, Zachary Cripps, Noah Fletcher, Enoch Gould, Zebulon Cunninghame, Seth Smith, Peleg Bucke, Gercyon Bucke (Gershom), Rachell Saunders, Lea Saunders, Calebb Carr, Jonathan Franklin, Boaz Sharpe, Esau del a Ware, Pharaoh Flinton, Othniell Haggat, Mordecay Knight, Obediah Hawes, Gamaliell Ellis, Esaias Raughton, Azarias Pinney, Elisha Mallowes, Malachi Mallock, Jonadab Illett, Joshua Long, Enecha Fitch (seemingly a feminine of Enoch), and Job Perridge. Occasionally an Epenetus Olney, or Nathaniell Patient, or Epaphroditus Haughton, or Cornelius Conway, or Feleaman Dickerson (Philemon), or Theophilus Lucas, or Annanias Mann is met with; but these are few, and were evidently selected for their size, the temptation to poach on apostolic preserves being too great when such big game was to be obtained. Besides, they were not in the calendar! These names went to Virginia, and they are not forgotten.

III. Objectionable Scripture Names.

Camden says—

"In times of Christianity, the names of most holy and vertuous persons, and of their most worthy progenitors, were given to stirre up men to the imitation of them, whose names they bare. But succeeding ages, little regarding St. Chrysostome's admonition to the contrary, have recalled prophane names, so as now Diana, Cassandra, Hyppolitus, Venus, Lais, names of unhappy disastre, are as rife somewhere, as ever they were in Paganisme."—"Remaines," p. 43.

The most cursory survey of our registers proves this. Captain Hercules Huncks and Ensign Neptune Howard fought under the Earl of Northumberland in 1640 (Peacock's "Army List of Roundheads and Cavaliers"). Both were Royalists.

"1643, Feb. 6. Buried Paris, son of William and Margaret Lee."—St. Michael, Spurriergate, York.

"1670, March 13. Baptized Cassandra, d. of James Smyth."—Banbury.

"1679, July 2. Buried Cassandra, ye wife of Edward Williams."—St. Michael, Barbados, (Hotten).

"1631, May 26. Married John Cotton and Venus Levat."—St. Peter, Cornhill.

Cartwright, the great Puritan, attacked these names in 1575, as "savouring of paganism" (Neal, v. p. xv. Appendix). It was a pity he did not include some names in the list of his co-religionists, for surely Tamar and Dinah were just as objectionable as Venus or Lais. The doctrine of a fallen nature could be upheld, and the blessed state of self-abasement maintained, without a daily reminder in the shape of a Bible name of evil repute. Bishop Corbett brought it as a distinct charge against the Puritans, that they loved to select the most unsavoury stories of Old Testament history for their converse. In the "Maypole" he makes a zealot minister say—

"To challenge liberty and recreation,
Let it be done in holy contemplation.
Brothers and sisters in the fields may walk,
Beginning of the Holy Word to talk:
Of David and Uria's lovely wife,
Of Tamar and her lustful brother's strife."

One thing is certain, these names became popular:

"1610, March. Baptized Bathsheba, d. of John Hamond, of Ratcliffe."—Stepney.

"1672, Feb. 23. Buried Bathsheba, wife of Richard Brinley, hosier."—St. Denis Backchurch.

The alternate form of Bath-shua (1 Chron. iii. 5) was used, although the clerks did not always know how to spell it:

"1609, July 1. Baptized Bathshira and Tabitha, daughters of Sir Antonie Dering, Knight."

"1609, July 5. Buried Bathshira and Tabitha, ds. of Sir Antonie Dering, Knight, being twines."—Pluckley, Kent.

"1601, Jan. Baptized Thamar, d. of Henry Reynold."—Stepney.

"1691, Nov. 20. Baptized Tamar, d. of Francis and Tamar Lee."—St. Dionis Backchurch.

"1698, April 10. Buried Tamar, wife of Richard Robinson, of Fell-foot."—Cartmel.

As for Dinah, she became a great favourite from her first introduction; every register contains her name before Elizabeth's death:

"1585, Aug. 15. Christening of Dina, d. of John Lister, barbor."

"1591, Aug. 21. Buried Mrs. Dina Walthall, a vertuous yong woman, 30 years."—St. Peter, Cornhill.

Crossing the Atlantic with the Pilgrim Fathers, she settled down at length as the typical negress; yet Puritan writers admitted that when she "went out to see the daughters of the land," she meant to be seen of the sons also!

Taylor, the Water-poet, seems to imply that Goliath was registered at baptism by the Puritan:

"Quoth he, 'what might the child baptized be?
Was it a male She, or a female He?'—
'I know not what, but 'tis a Son,' she said.—
'Nay then,' quoth he, 'a wager may be laid
It had some Scripture name.'—'Yes, so it had,'
Said she: 'but my weak memory's so bad,
I have forgot it: 'twas a godly name,
Tho' out of my remembrance be the same:
'Twas one of the small prophets verily:
'Twas not Esaias, nor yet Jeremy,
Ezekiel, Daniel, nor good Obadiah,
Ah, now I do remember, 'twas Goliah!'"

Pharaoh occurs, and went out to Virginia, where it has ever since remained. It is, as already shown, familiar enough in Yorkshire.

Of New Testament names, whose associations are of evil repute, we may mention Ananias, Sapphira, and Antipas. Ananias had become so closely connected with Puritanism, that not only did Dryden poke fun at the relationship in the "Alchemist," but Ananias Dulman became the cant term for a long-winded zealot preacher. So says Neal.

"1603, Sep. 12. Buried Ananias, sonne of George Warren, 17 years."—St. Peter, Cornhill.

"1621, Sep. Baptized Ananias, son of Ananias Jarratt, glassmaker."—Stepney.

Sapphira occurs in Bunhill Fields:

"Here lyeth the body of Mrs. Sapphira Lightmaker, wife of Mr. Edward Lightmaker, of Broadhurst, in Sussex, gent. She died in the Lorde, Dec. 20, 1704, aged 81 years."

She was therefore born in 1633. Her brother (they were brought up Presbyterians) was Robert Leighton, who died Archbishop of Glasgow.

Drusilla, again, was objectionable, but perchance her character was less historically known then:

"1622. Baptized Drusilla, d. of Thomas Davis."—Ludlow.

Antipas, curiously enough, was almost popular, although a murderer and an adulterer:

"1633, Feb. 28. Baptized Antipas, sonne of Robert Barnes, of Shadwell."—Stepney.

"1662. Petition of Antipas Charrington."—"Cal. St. P. Dom."

"1650. Antipas Swinnerton, Tedbury, wollman."—"Tokens of Seventeenth Century."

Dr. Increase Mather, the eminent Puritan, in his work entitled "Remarkable Providences," published at Boston, U.S.A., in 1684, has a story of an interposition in behalf of his friend Antipas Newman.

Of other instances, somewhat later, Sehon Stace, who lived in Warding in 1707 ("Suss. Arch. Coll.," xii. 254), commemorates the King of the Amorites, Milcom Groat ("Cal. St. P.," 1660) representing on English soil "the abomination of the children of Ammon." Dr. Pusey and Mr. Spurgeon might be excused a little astonishment at such a conversion by baptism.

Barrabas cannot be considered a happy choice:

"Buried, 1713, Oct. 18, Barabas, sonne of Barabas Bowen."—All-Hallows, Barking.

Mr. Maskell draws attention to the name in his history of that church. There is something so emphatic about "now Barrabas was a robber," that thoughts of theft seem proper to the very name. We should have locked up the spoons, we feel sure, had father or son called upon us. The father who called his son "Judas-not-Iscariot" scarcely cleared the name of its evil associations, nor would it quite meet the difficulty suggested by the remark in "Tristram Shandy:"

"Your Billy, sir—would you for the world have called him Judas?... Would you, sir, if a Jew of a godfather had proposed the name of your child, and offered you his purse along with it—would you have consented to such a desecration of him?"

We have all heard the story of Beelzebub. If the child had been inadvertently so baptized, a remedy might have been found in former days by changing the name at confirmation. Until 1552, the bishop confirmed by name. Archbishop Peccham laid down a rule:

"The minister shall take care not to permit wanton names, which being pronounced do sound to lasciviousness, to be given to children baptized, especially of the female sex: and if otherwise it be done, the same shall be changed by the bishop at confirmation."

That this law had been carelessly followed after the Reformation is clear, else Venus Levat, already quoted, would not have been married in 1631 under that name. Certainly Dinah and Tamar come under the ban of this injunction.

Curiously enough, the change of name was sanctioned in the case of orthodox names, for Lord Coke says—

"If a man be baptized by the name of Thomas, and after, at his confirmation by the Bishop, he is named John, his name of confirmation shall stand."

He then quotes the case of Sir Francis Gawdie, Chief Justice of the Court of Common Pleas, whose name by baptism was Thomas, Thomas being changed to Francis at confirmation. He holds that Francis shall stand ("Institutes," 1. iii.). This practice manifestly arose out of Peccham's rule, but it is strange that wanton instances should be left unchanged, and the orthodox allowed to be altered.

Arising out of the Puritan error of permitting names like Tamar and Dinah to stand, modern eccentricity has gone very far, and it would be satisfactory to see many names in use at present forbidden. I need not quote the Venuses of our directories. Emanuel is of an opposite character, and should be considered blasphemy. We have not adopted Christ yet, as Dr. Doran reminded us they have done in Germany, but my copy of the London Directory shows at least one German, bearing the baptismal name of Christ, at present dwelling in the metropolis. Puritan eccentricity is a trifle to this.

IV. Losses.

(a.) The Destruction of Pet Forms.

But let us now notice some of the more disastrous effects of the great Hebrew invasion. The most important were the partial destruction of the nick forms, and the suppression of diminutives. The English pet names disappeared, never more to return. Desinences in "cock," "kin," "elot," "ot," "et," "in," and "on," are no more found in current literature, nor in the clerk's register. Why should this be so? An important reason strikes us at once. The ecclesiastic names on which the enclytics had grown had become unpopular well-nigh throughout England. It was an English, not a Puritan prejudice. With the suppression of the names proper went the desinences attached to them. The tree being felled, the parasite decayed. Another reason was this: the names introduced from the Scriptures did not seem to compound comfortably with these terminatives. The Hebrew name would first have to be turned into a nick form before the diminutive was appended. The English peasantry had added "in," "ot," "kin," and "cock" only to the nickname, never to the baptismal form. It was Wat-kin, not Walterkin; Bat-kin, not Bartholomewkin; Wilcock, not Williamcock; Colin, not Nicholas-in; Philpot, not Philipot. But the popular feeling for a century was against turning the new Scripture names into curt nick forms. As it would have been an absurdity to have appended diminutives to sesquipedalian names, national wit, rather than deliberate plan, prevented it. If it was irreverent, too, to curtail Scripture names, it was equally irreverent to give them the diminutive dress. To prove the absolute truth of my statement, I have only to remind the reader that, saving "Nat-kin," not one single Bible name introduced by the Reformation and the English Bible has become conjoined with a diminutive.

The immediate consequence was this; the diminutive forms became obsolete. Emmott lingered on till the end of the seventeenth century; nay, got into the eighteenth:

"Emmit, d. of Edward and Ann Buck, died 24 April, 1726, aged 6 years."—Hawling, Gloucester.

But it was only where it was not known as a form of Emma, and possibly both might exist in the same household. I have already furnished instances of Hamlet. Here is another:

"The Rev. Hamlet Marshall, D.D., died in the Close, Lincoln, in 1652. With him dwelt his nephew, Hamlet Joyce. He bequeaths legacies in his will to Hamlet Pickerin and Hamlet Duncalf, and his executor was his son, Hamlet Marshall."—Notes and Queries, February 14, 1880.

It lasted till the eighteenth century. But nobody knew by that time that it was a pet name of Hamon, or Hamond; nay, few knew that the surname of Hammond had ever been a baptismal name at all:

"1620, Jan. 3. Buried Hamlet Rigby, Mr. Askew's man."—St. Peter, Cornhill.

"1620. Petition of Hamond Franklin."—"Cal. S. P. Dom.," 1619-1623.

It is curious to notice that Mr. Hovenden, in his "Canterbury Register," published 1878, for the

Harleian Society, has the following entries:—

"1627, Aprill 3. Christened Ham'on, the sonn of Richard Struggle."

"1634. Jan. 18. Christened Damaris, daughter of Mr. Ham'on Leucknor."

Turning to the index, the editor has styled them Hamilton Struggle and Hamilton Leucknor. Ham'on, of course, is Hammon, or Hammond. I may add that some ecclesiastic, a critic of my book on "English Surnames," in the Guardian, rebuked me for supposing that Emmot could be from Emma, and calmly put it down as a form of Aymot! What can prove the effect of the Reformation on old English names as do such incidents as these?

An English monarch styled his favourite Peter Gaveston as "Piers," a form that was sufficiently familiar to readers of history; but when an antiquary, some few years ago, found this same Gaveston described as "Perot," it became a difficulty to not a few. The Perrots or Parratts of our London Directory might have told them of the old-fashioned diminutive that had been knocked on the head with a Hebrew Bible.

Collet, from Nicholas, used as a feminine name, died out also. The last instance I know of is—

"1629, Jan. 15. Married Thomas Woollard and Collatt Hargrave."—St. Peter, Cornhill.

Colin, the other pet form, having got into our pastoral poetry, lingered longer, and may be said to be still alive:

"1728. Married Colin Foster and Beulah Digby."—Somerset House Chapel.

The last Wilmot I have discovered is a certain Wilmote Adams, a defendant in a Chancery suit at the end of Elizabeth's reign ("Chancery Suits: Elizabeth"), and the last Philpot is dated 1575:

"1575, Aug. 26. Christened Philpott, a chylde that was laide at Mr Alderman Osberne's gatt."—St. Dionis Backchurch.

All the others perished by the time James I. was king. Guy, or Wyatt, succumbed entirely, and the same may be said of the rest. Did we require further confirmation of this, I need only inquire: Would any Yorkshireman now, as he reads over shop-fronts in towns like Leeds or Bradford, or in the secluded villages of Wensleydale or Swaledale, the surnames of Tillot and Tillotson, Emmett and Emmotson, Ibbott, Ibbet, Ibbs, and Ibbotson, know that, twenty years before the introduction of our English Bible, these were not merely the familiar pet names of Matilda, Emma, and Isabella, but that as a trio they stood absolutely first in the scale of frequency? Nay, they comprised more than forty-five per cent. of the female population.

The last registered Ibbot or Issot I have seen is in the Chancery suits at the close of Queen Bess's reign, wherein Ibote Babyngton and Izott Barne figure in some legal squabbles ("Chancery Suits: Elizabeth," vol. ii.). As for Sissot, or Drewet, or Doucet, or Fawcett, or Hewet, or Philcock, or Jeffcock, or Batkin, or Phippin, or Lambin, or Perrin, they have passed away— their place knoweth them no more. What a remarkable revolution is this, and so speedy!

Failing our registers, the question may arise whether or not in familiar converse the old pet forms were still used. Our ballads and plays preserve many of the nick forms, but scarcely a pet form is to be seen later than 1590. In 1550 Nicholas Udall wrote "Ralph Roister Doister," in the very commencement of which Matthew Merrygreek "says or sings"—

"Sometime Lewis Loiterer biddeth me come near:

Somewhiles Watkin Waster maketh us good cheer."

Amongst the dramatis personæ are Dobinet Doughty, Sim Suresby, Madge Mumblecrust, Tibet Talkapace, and Annot Aliface. A few years later came "Gammer Gurton's Needle." Both Diccon and Hodge figure in it: two rustics of the most bucolic type. Hodge, after relating how Gib the cat had licked the milk-pan clean, adds—

"Gog's souls, Diccon, Gib our cat had eat the bacon too."

Immediately after this, again, in 1568 was printed "Like will to Like." The chief characters are Tom Tosspot, Hankin Hangman, Pierce Pickpurse, and Nichol Newfangle. Wat Waghalter is also introduced. But here may be said to end this homely and contemporary class of play-names. 'Tis true, in Beaumont and Fletcher's "Beggar's Bush," Higgen (Higgin) is one of the "three knavish beggars," but the scene is laid in Flanders.

Judging by our songs and comedies, the diminutive forms went down with terrible rapidity, and were practically obsolete before Elizabeth's death. But this result was more the work of the Reformation at large than Puritanism.

(b.) The Decrease of Nick Forms.

This was not all. The nick forms saw themselves reduced to straits. The new godly names, I have said, were not to be turned into irreverent cant terms. From the earliest day of the Reformation every man who gave his child a Bible name stuck to it unaltered. Ebenezer at baptism was Ebenezer among the turnips, Ebenezer with the milk-pail, and Ebenezer in courtship; while Deborah, who did not become Deb till Charles I.'s reign, would Ebenezer him till the last day she had done scolding him, and put "Ebenezer" carefully on his grave, to prove how happily they had lived together!

As for the zealot who gradually forged his way to the front, he gave his brother and sister in the Lord the full benefit of his or her title, whether it was five syllables or seven. There can be no doubt that these Hebrew names did not readily adapt themselves to ordinary converse with the world. Melchisedek and Ebedmelech were all right elbowing their way into the conventicle, but Melchisedek dispensing half-pounds of butter over the counter, or Ebedmelech carrying milk-pails from door to door, gave people a kind of shock. These grand assumptions suggested knavery. One feels certain that our great-grandmothers had a suspicion of tallow in the butter, and Jupiter Pluvius in the pail.

Nor did these excavated names harmonize with the surnames to which they were yoked. Adoniram was quaint enough without Byfield, but both (as Butler, in "Hudibras," knew) suggested something slightly ludicrous. Byron took a mean advantage of this when he attacked poor Cottle, the bookseller and would-be writer:

"O Amos Cottle! Phœbus! what a name

To fill the speaking trump of future fame!

O Amos Cottle! for a moment think

What meagre profits spring from pen and ink."

Amos is odd, but Amos united to Cottle makes a smile irresistible.

Who does not agree with Wilkes, who, when speaking to Johnson of Dryden's would-be rival, the city poet, says—

"Elkanah Settle sounds so queer, who can expect much from that name? We should have no hesitation to give it for John Dryden, in preference to Elkanah Settle, from the names only, without knowing their different merits"?

And Sterne, as the elder Disraeli reminds us, in one of his multitudinous digressions from the life of "Tristram Shandy," makes the progenitor of that young gentleman turn absolutely melancholy, as he conjures up a vision of all the men who

"might have done exceeding well in the world, had not their characters and spirits been totally depressed, and Nicodemas'd into nothing."

Even Oliver Goldsmith cannot resist styling the knavish seller of green spectacles by a conjunction of Hebrew and English titles as Ephraim Jenkinson; and his servant, who acts the part of a Job Trotter (another Old Testament worthy, again) to his master, is, of course, Abraham!

But, oddly as such combinations strike upon the modern tympanum, what must not the effect have been in a day when a nickname was popular according as it was curt? How would men rub their eyes in sheer amazement, when such conjunctions as Ebedmelech Gastrell, or Epaphroditus Haughton, or Onesiphorus Dixey, were introduced to their notice, pronounced with all sesquipedalian fulness, following upon the very heels of a long epoch of traditional one-syllabled Ralphs, Hodges, Hicks, Wats, Phips, Bates, and Balls (Baldwin). Conceive the amazement at such registrations as these:

"1599, Sep. 23. Christened Aholiab, sonne of Michaell Nicolson, cordwainer."—St. Peter, Cornhill.

"1569, June 1. Christened Ezekiell, sonne of Robert Pownall."—Cant. Cath.

"1582, April 1. Christened Melchisadeck, sonne of Melchizadeck Bennet, poulter."—St. Peter, Cornhill.

"1590, Dec. 20. Christened Abacucke, sonne of John Tailer."—Ditto.

"1595, Nov. Christened Zabulon, sonne of John Griffin."—Stepney.

"1603, Sep. 15. Buried Melchesideck King."—Cant. Cath.

"1645, July 19. Buried Edward, sonne of Mephibosheth Robins."—St. Peter, Cornhill.

"1660, Nov. 5. Buried Jehostiaphat (sic) Star."—Cant. Cath.

"1611, Oct. 21. Baptized Zipporah, d. of Richard Beere, of Wapping."—Stepney.

The "Chancery Suits" of Elizabeth contain a large batch of such names; and I have already enumerated a list of "Pilgrim Fathers" of James's reign, whose baptisms would be recorded in the previous century.

But compare this with the fact that the leading men in England at this very time were recognized only by the curtest of abbreviated names. In that very quaint poem of Heywood's, "The Hierarchie of Blessed Angels," the author actually makes it the ground of an affected remonstrance:

"Marlowe, renowned for his rare art and wit,
Could ne'er attain beyond the name of Kit,

Although his Hero and Leander did
Merit addition rather. Famous Kid
Was called but Tom. Tom Watson, though he wrote
Able to make Apollo's self to dote
Upon his muse, for all that he could strive,
Yet never could to his full name arrive.
Tom Nash, in his time of no small esteem,
Could not a second syllable redeem.
....

Mellifluous Shakespeare, whose enchanting quill
Commanded mirth or passion, was but Will:
And famous Jonson, though his learned pen
Be dipped in Castaly, is still but Ben."
However, in the end, he attributes the familiarity to the right cause:
"I, for my part,
Think others what they please, accept that heart
That courts my love in most familiar phrase;
And that it takes not from my pains or praise,
If any one to me so bluntly come:
I hold he loves me best that calls me Tom."
It is Sir Christopher, the curate, who, in "The Ordinary," rebels against "Kit:"
"Andrew. What may I call your name, most reverend sir?
Bagshot. His name's Sir Kit.
Christopher. My name is not so short:
'Tis a trisyllable, an't please your worship;
But vulgar tongues have made bold to profane it
With the short sound of that unhallowed idol
They call a kit. Boy, learn more reverence!
Bagshot. Yes, to my betters."
We need not wonder, therefore, that the comedists took their fun out of the new custom,
especially in relation to their length and pronunciation in full. In Cowley's "Cutter of Colman
Street," Cutter turns Puritan, and thus addresses the colonel's widow, Tabitha:
"Sister Barebottle, I must not be called Cutter any more: that is a name of Cavalier's darkness;
the Devil was a Cutter from the beginning: my name is now Abednego: I had a vision which
whispered to me through a key-hole, 'Go, call thyself Abednego.'"
In his epilogue to this same comedy, Cutter is supposed to address the audience as a
"congregation of the elect," the playhouse is a conventicle, and he is a "pious cushion-thumper."
Gazing about the theatre, he says—through his nose, no doubt—
"But yet I wonder much not to espy a
Brother in all this court called Zephaniah."

This is a better rhyme even than Butler's

"Their dispensations had been stifled
But for our Adoniram Byfield."

In Brome's "Covent Garden Weeded," the arrival at the vintner's door is thus described:

"Rooksbill. Sure you mistake him, sir.
Vintner. You are welcome, gentlemen: Will, Harry, Zachary!
Gabriel. Zachary is a good name.
Vintner. Where are you? Shew up into the Phoenix."—Act. ii. sc. 2.

The contrast between Will or Harry, the nick forms, and Zachary, the full name, is intentionally drawn, and Gabriel instantly rails at it.

In "Bartholomew Fair," half the laughter that convulsed Charles II., his courtiers, and courtezans, was at the mention of Ezekiel, the cut-purse, or Zeal-of-the-land, the baker, who saw visions; while the veriest noodle in the pit saw the point of Squire Cokes' perpetually addressing his body-man Humphrey in some such style as this:

"O, Numps! are you here, Numps? Look where I am, Numps, and Mistress Grace, too! Nay, do not look so angrily, Numps: my sister is here and all, I do not come without her."

How the audience would laugh and cheer at a sally that was simply manufactured of a repetition of the good old-fashioned name for Humphrey; and thus a passage that reads as very dull fun indeed to the ears of the nineteenth century, would seem to be brimful of sarcastic allusion to the popular audience of the seventeenth, especially when spoken by such lips as Wintersels.

The same effect was attempted and attained in the "Alchemist." Subtle addresses the deacon:

"What's your name?
Ananias. My name is Ananias.
Subtle.Out, the varlet
That cozened the Apostles! Hence away!
Flee, mischief! had your holy consistory
No name to send me, of another sound,
Than wicked Ananias? Send your elders
Hither, to make atonement for you, quickly,
And give me satisfaction: or out goes
The fire ...
If they stay threescore minutes; the aqueity,
Terreity, and sulphureity
Shall run together again, and all be annulled,
Thou wicked Ananias!"

Exit Ananias, and no wonder. Of course, the pit would roar at the expense of Ananias. But Abel, the tobacco-man, who immediately appears in his place, is addressed familiarly as "Nab:"

"Face. Abel, thou art made.
Abel. Sir, I do thank his worship.

Face. Six o' thy legs more will not do it, Nab.

He has brought you a pipe of tobacco, doctor.

Abel. Yes, sir; I have another thing I would impart——

Face. Out with it, Nab.

Abel.Sir, there is lodged hard by me

A rich young widow."

To some readers there will be little point in this. They will say "Abel," as an Old Testament name, should neither have been given to an un-puritanic character, nor ought it to have been turned into a nickname. This would never have occurred to the audience. Abel, or Nab, had been one of the most popular of English names for at least three centuries before the Reformation. Hence it was never used by the Puritans, and was, as a matter of course, the undisturbed property of their enemies. Three centuries of bad company had ruined Nab's morals. The zealot would none of it.

But from all this it will be seen that a much better fight was made in behalf of the old nick forms than of the diminutives. By a timely rally, Tom, Jack, Dick, and Harry were carried, against all hindrances, into the Restoration period, and from that time they were safe. Wat, Phip, Hodge, Bat or Bate, and Cole lost their position, but so had the fuller Philip, Roger, Bartholomew, and Nicholas, But the opponents of Puritanism carried the war into the enemy's camp in revenge for this, and Priscilla, Deborah, Jeremiah, and Nathaniel, although they were rather of the Reformation than Puritanic introductions, were turned by the time of Charles I. into the familiar nick forms of Pris, Deb, Jerry, and Nat. The licentious Richard Brome, in "The New Academy," even attempts a curtailment of Nehemiah:

"Lady Nestlecock. Negh, Negh!

Nehemiah. Hark! my mother comes.

Lady N. Where are you, childe? Negh!

Nehemiah. I hear her neighing after me."

Act iv. sc. 1. (1658).

It was never tried out of doors, however, and the experiment was not repeated. Brome was still more scant in reverence to Damaris. In "Covent Garden Weeded" Madge begins "the dismal story:"

"This gentlewoman whose name is Damaris——

Nich. Damyris, stay: her nickname then is Dammy: so we may call her when we grow familiar; and to begin that familiarity—Dammy, here's to you. (Drinks.)"

After this she is Dammy in the mouth of Nicholas throughout the play. This, too, was a failure. Indeed, it demonstrates a remarkable reverence for their Bible on the part of the English race, that every attempt to turn one of its names into a nick form (saving in some three or four instances) has ignominiously failed. We mean, of course, since the Reformation.

The Restoration was a great restoration of nick forms. Such names as had survived were again for a while in full favour, and the reader has only to turn to the often coarse ballads and songs contained in such collections as Tom d'Urfey's "Pills to Purge Melancholy" to see how Nan, Sis,

Sib, Kate, and Doll had been brought back to popular favour. It was but a spurt, however, in the main. As the lascivious reaction from the Puritanic strait-lacedness in some degree spent itself, so did the newly restored fashion, and when the eighteenth century brought in a fresh innovation, viz. the classic forms, such as Beatrix, Maria, Lætitia, Carolina, Louisa, Amelia, Georgina, Dorothea, Prudentia, Honora—an innovation that for forty years ran like an epidemic through every class of society, and was sarcastically alluded to by Goldsmith in Miss Carolina Wilhelmina Amelia Skeggs, and the sisters Olivia and Sophia—the old nick forms once more bade adieu to English society, and now enjoy but a partial favour. But Bill, Tom, Dick, and Harry still hold on like grim death. Long may they continue to do so!

(c.) The Decay of Saint and Festival Names.

There were some serious losses in hagiology. Names that had figured in the calendar for centuries fared badly; Simon, Peter, Nicholas, Bartholomew, Philip, and Matthew, from being first favourites, lapsed into comparative oblivion. Some virgins and martyrs of extra-Biblical repute, like Agnes, Ursula, Catharine, Cecilia, or Blaze, crept into the registers of Charles's reign, but they had then become but shadows of their former selves.

'Sis' is often found in D'Urfey's ballads, but it only proves the songs themselves were old ones, or at any rate the choruses, for Cecilia was practically obsolete:

"1574, Oct. 8. Buried Cisly Weanewright, ye carter's wife."—St. Peter, Cornhill.

"1578, June 1. Buried Cissellye, wife of Gilles Lambe."—St. Dionis Backchurch.

"1547, Dec. 26. Married Thomas Bodnam and Urcylaye Watsworth."—Ditto.

"1654, Sep. 20. Buried Ursley, d. of John Fife."—St. Peter, Cornhill.

It was now that Awdry gave way:

"1576, Sept. 7. Buryed Awdry, the widow of — Seward."—St. Peter, Cornhill.

"1610, May 27. Baptized Awdrey, d. of John Cooke, butcher."—St. Dionis Backchurch.

St. Blaze, the patron saint of wool-combers and the nom-de-plume of Gil Blas, has only a church or two to recall his memory to us now. But he lived into Charles's reign:

"Blaze Winter was master of Stodmarsh Hospital, when it was surrendered to Queen Elizabeth, 1575."—Hasted's "History of Kent."

"1550, May 23. Baptized Blaze, daughter of — Goodwinne."—St. Peter, Cornhill.

"1555, Julie 21. Wedding of Blase Sawlter and Collis Smith."—Ditto.

"1662, May 6. Blase Whyte, one of ye minor cannons, to Mrs. Susanna Wright, widow."—Cant. Cath.

This is the last instance I have seen. Hillary shared the same fate:

"1547, Jan. 30. Married Hillarye Finch and Jane Whyte."—St. Dionis Backchurch.

"1557, June 27. Wedding of Hillary Wapolle and Jane Garret."—St. Peter, Cornhill.

"1593, Jan. 20. Christening of Hillary, sonne of Hillary Turner, draper."—Ditto.

Bride is rarely found in England now:

"1556, May 22. Baptized Bryde, daughter of — Stoakes."

"1553, Nov. 27. Baptized Bryde, daughter of — Faunt."—St. Peter, Cornhill.

Benedict, which for three hundred years had been known as Bennet, as several London churches can testify, became well-nigh extinct; but the feminine Benedicta, with Bennet for its shortened form, suddenly arose on its ashes, and flourished for a time:

"1517, Jan. 28. Wedding of William Stiche and Bennet Bennet, widow."—St. Peter, Cornhill.

"1653, Sep. 29. Married Richard Moone to Benedicta Rolfe."—Cant. Cath.

"1575, Jan. 25. Baptized Bennett, son of John Langdon."—St. Columb Major.

These feminines are sometimes bothering. Look, for instance, at this:

"1596, Feb. 6. Wedding of William Bromley and Mathew Barnet, maiden, of this parish."—St. Peter, Cornhill.

"1655, Sep. 24. Married Thomas Budd, miller, and Mathew Larkin, spinster."—Ditto.

The true spelling should have been Mathea, which, previous to the Reformation, had been given to girls born on St. Matthew's Day. The nick form Mat changed sexes. In "Englishmen for my Money" Walgrave says—

"Nay, stare not, look you here: no monster I, But even plain Ned, and here stands Mat my wife."

Appoline, all of whose teeth were extracted at her martyrdom with pincers, was a favourite saint for appeal against toothache. In the Homily "Against the Perils of Idolatry," it is said—

"All diseases have their special saints, as gods, the curers of them: the toothache, St. Appoline."

Scarcely any name for girls was more common than this for a time; up to the Commonwealth period it contrived to exist. Take St. Peter, Cornhill, alone:

"1593, Jan. 13. Christened Apeline, d. of John Moris, clothworker.

"1609, Mch. 11. Christened Apoline, d. of Willm. Burton, marchant.

"1617, June 29. Buried Appelyna, d. of Thomas Church."

Names from the great Church festivals fared as badly as those from the hagiology. The high day of the ecclesiastical calendar is Easter. We have more relics of this festival than any other. Pasche Oland or Pascoe Kerne figure in the Chancery suits of Elizabeth. Long before this the Hundred Rolls had given us a Huge fil. Pasche, and a contemporary record contained an Antony Pascheson. The different forms lingered till the Commonwealth:

"1553, Mch. 23. Baptized Pascall, son of John Davye."—St. Dionis Backchurch.

"1651, Mch. 18. Married Thomas Strato and Paskey Prideaux."—St. Peter's, Cornhill.

"1747, May 4. Baptized Rebekah, d. of Pasko and Sarah Crocker."—St. Dionis Backchurch.

"1582, June 14. Baptized Pascow, son-in-law of Pascowe John."—St. Columb Major.

Pascha Turner, widow, was sister of Henry Parr, Bishop of Worcester.

The more English "Easter" had a longer survival, but this arose from its having become confounded with Esther. To this mistake it owes the fact that it lived till the commencement of the present century:

"April, 1505. Christened Easter, daughter of Thomas Coxe, of Wapping."—Stepney.

"May 27, 1764. Buried Easter Lewis, aged 56 years."—Lidney, Glouc.

"July 27, 1654. Married Thomas Burton, marriner, and Easter Taylor."—St. Peter, Cornhill.

Epiphany, or Theophania (shortened to Tiffany), was popular with both sexes, but the ladies got the chief hold of it.

"Megge Merrywedyr, and Sabyn Sprynge,
Tiffany Twynkeler, fayle for no thynge,"

says one of our old mysteries. This form succumbed at the Reformation. Tyffanie Seamor appears as defendant about 1590, however ("Chancery Suits: Eliz."), and in Cornwall the name reached the seventeenth century:

"1594, Nov. 7. Baptized Typhenie, daughter of Sampson Bray.

"1600, June 21. Baptized Tiffeny, daughter of Harry Hake."—St. Columb Major.

The following is from Banbury register:

"1586, Jan. 9. Baptized Epiphane, ye sonne of Ambrose Bentley."

Epiphany Howarth records his name also about 1590 ("Chancery Suits: Eliz."), and a few years later he is once more met with in a State paper (C. S. P. 1623-25):

"1623, June. Account of monies paid by Epiphan Haworth, of Herefordshire, recusant, since Nov. 11, 1611, £6 10 0."

This Epiphan is valuable as showing the transition state between Epiphania and Ephin, the latter being the form that ousted all others:

"1563, March 14. Christening of Ephin King, d. of — King.

"1564, June 30. Christening of Effam, d. of John Adlington.

"1620, March 30. Frauncis, sonne of Alexander Brounescome, and Effym, his wife, brought a bead at Mr. Vowell's house.

"1635, Jan. 28. Buried Epham Vowell, widow."—St. Peter, Cornhill.

But Ephin was not a long liver, and by the time of the Restoration had wholly succumbed. The last entry I have seen is in the Westminster Abbey register:

"1692, Jan. 25. Buried Eppifania Cakewood, an almsman's wife."

Pentecost was more sparely used. In the "Rotuli Litterarum Clausarum in Turri Londonensi" occur both Pentecost de London (1221) and Pentecost Servicus, and a servitor of Henry III. bore the only name of "Pentecost" ("Inquis., 13 Edw. I.," No. 13). This name was all but obsolete soon after the Reformation set in, but it lingered on till the end of the seventeenth century.

"1577, May 25. Baptized Pentecost, daughter of Robert Rosegan."—St. Columb Major.

"1610, May 27. Baptized Pentecost, d. of William Tremain."—Ditto.

"August 7, 1696. Pentecost, daughter of Mr. Ezekel and Pentecost Hall, merchant, born and baptized."—St. Dionis Backchurch.

Noel shared the same fate. The Hundred Rolls furnish a Noel de Aubianis, while the "Materials for a History of Henry VII." (p. 503) mentions a Nowell Harper:

"1486, July 16. General pardon to Nowell Harper, late of Boyleston, co. Derby, gent."

"1545, Dec. 20. Baptized Nowell, son of William Mayhowe."—St. Columb Major.

"1580, March 1. Baptized James, son of Nowell Mathew."—Ditto.

"1627. Petition of Nowell Warner."—"C. S. P. Domestic," 1627-8.

Noel still struggled gamely, and died hard, seeing the eighteenth century well in:

"1706, April 23. Noell Whiteing, son of Noell and Ann Whiteing, linendraper, baptized."—St.

Dionis Backchurch.

Again the Reformation, apart from Puritanism, had much to do with the decay of these names.
(d.) The Last of some Old Favourites.

There were some old English favourites that the Reformation and the English Bible did not immediately crush. Thousands of men were youths when the Hebrew invasion set in, and lived unto James's reign. Their names crop up, of course, in the burial registers. Others were inclined to be tenacious over family favourites. We must be content, in the records of Elizabeth's and even James's reign, to find some old friends standing side by side with the new. The majority of them were extra-Biblical, and therefore did not meet with the same opposition as those that savoured of the old ecclesiasticism. Nevertheless, this new fashion was telling on them, and of most we may say, "Their places know them no more."

Looking from now back to then, we see this the more clearly. We turn to the "Calendar of State Papers," and we find a grant, dated November 5, 1607, to Fulk Reade to travel four years. Shortly afterwards (July 15, 1609), we come across a warrant to John Carse, of the benefit of the recusancy of Drew Lovett, of the county of Middlesex. Casting our eye backwards we speedily reach a grant or warrant in 1603, wherein Gavin Harvey is mentioned. In 1604 comes Ingram Fyser. One after another these names occur within the space of five years—names then, although it was well in James's reign, known of all men, and borne reputably by many. But who will say that Drew, or Fulk, or Gavin, or Ingram are alive now? How they were to be elbowed out of existence these very same records tell us; for within the same half-decade we may see warrants or grants relating to Matathias Mason (April 7, 1610) or Gersome Holmes (January 23, 1608). Jethro Forstall obtains licence, November 12, 1604, to dwell in one of the alms-rooms of Canterbury Cathedral; while Melchizedec Bradwood receives sole privilege, February 18, 1608, of printing Jewel's "Defence of the Apology of the English Church." The enemy was already within the bastion, and the call for surrender was about to be made.

Take another specimen a few years earlier. In the Chancery suits at the close of Elizabeth's reign, we find a plaintiff named Goddard Freeman, another styled Anketill Brasbridge, a defendant bearing the good old title of Frideswide Heysham, while a fourth endeavours to secure his title to some property under the signature of Avery Howlatt. Hamlett Holcrofte and Hammett Hyde are to be met with (but we have spoken of them), and such other personages as Ellice Heye, Morrice Cowles, and Gervase Hatfield. Within a few pages' limit we come across Dogory Garry, Digory Greenfield, Digory Harrit, and Degory Hollman. These names of Goddard, Anketill, Frideswide, Avery, Hamlet, Ellice, Morrice, Gervase, and Digory were on everybody's lips when Henry VIII. was king. Who can say that they exist now? Only Maurice and Gervase enjoy a precarious existence. A breath of popular disregard would blow them out. Avery held out, but in vain:

"Avery Terrill, cooke at ye Falcon, Lothbury, 1650."—"Tokens of Seventeenth Century."

But what else do we see in these same registers? We are confronted with pages bearing such names as Esaye Freeman (Isaiah), or Elizar Audly (Eliezer), or Seth Awcocke, or Urias Babington, or Ezekias Brent,—and this not forty years after the Reformation. These men must have been baptized in the very throes of the great contest.

Another "Calendar of State Papers," bearing dates between 1590 and 1605, contains the names of Colet Carey (1580) and Amice Carteret (1599), alongside of whom stands Aquila Wyke (1603). Here once more we are reminded of two pretty baptismal names that have gone the way of the others. It makes one quite sad to think of these national losses. Amice, previous to the Reformation, was a household favourite, and Colet a perfect pet. Won't somebody come to the rescue? Why on earth should the fact that the Bible has been translated out of Latin into English strip us of these treasures?

Turn once more to our church registers. Few will recognize Thurstan as a baptismal name:

"1544, May 11. Married Thryston Hogkyn and Letyce Knight."—St. Dionis Backchurch.

"1573, Nov. 15. Wedding of Thrustone Bufford and Annes Agnes Dyckson."—St. Peter, Cornhill.

Drew and Fulk are again found:

"1583, April 16. Buried Drew Hewat, sonne of Nicholas Hewat.

"1583, March 8. Buried Foulke Phillip, sonne of Thomas Phillip, grocer."—St. Peter, Cornhill.

Take the following, dropped upon hap-hazard as I turn the pages of St. Dionis Backchurch:

"1540, Oct. 25. Buried Jacomyn Swallowe.

"1543, Aug. 3. Buried Awdrye Hykman.

"1543, June 12. Married Bonyface Meorys and Jackamyn Kelderly.

"1546, Nov. 23. Christened Grizill, daughter of—Deyne.

"1557, Nov. 8. Buried Austin Clarke.

"1567, April 22. Married Richard Staper and Dennis Hewyt.

"1573, Sep. 25. Married John Carrington and Gyllian Lovelake.

"1574, Oct. 23. Buried Joyce, d. of John Bray.

"1594, Nov. 1. Married Gawyn Browne and Sibbell Halfhed."

So they run. How quaint and pretty they sound to modern ears! Amongst the above I have mentioned some girl-names. The change is strongly marked here. It was Elizabeth's reign saw the end of Joan. Jane Grey set the fashionable Jane going; Joan was relegated to the milkmaid, and very soon even the kitchen wench would none of it. Joan is obsolete; Jane is showing signs of dissolution.

It was Elizabeth's reign saw the end of Jill, or Gill, which had been the pet name of Juliana for three centuries:

"1586, Feb. 5. Christening of Gillian Jones, daughter of Thomas Jones, grocer."—St. Peter, Cornhill.

"1573, Sep. 25. Married John Carrington, Cheape, and Gillian Lovelake."—St. Dionis Backchurch.

In one of our earlier mysteries Noah's wife had refused to enter the ark. To Noah she had said—

"Sir, for Jak nor for Gille

Wille I turne my face,

Tille I have on this hille
Spun a space."
It lingered on till the close of James's reign. In 1619 we find in "Satyricall Epigrams"—
"Wille squabbled in a tavern very sore,
Because one brought a gill of wine—no more:
'Fill me a quart,' quoth he, 'I'm called Will;
The proverb is, each Jacke shall have his Gill.'"
But Jill had become a term for a common street jade, like Parnel and Nan. All these disappeared at this period, and must have sunk into disuse, Bible or no Bible. A nanny-house, or simple "nanny," was well known to the loose and dissolute of either sex at the close of the sixteenth century. Hence, in the ballad "The Two Angrie Women of Abington," Nan Lawson is a wanton; while, in "Slippery Will," the hero's inclination for Nan is anything but complimentary:
"Long have I lived a bachelor's life,
And had no mind to marry;
But now I faine would have a wife,
Either Doll, Kate, Sis, or Mary.
These four did love me very well,
I had my choice of Mary;
But one did all the rest excell,
And that was pretty Nanny.
"Sweet Nan did love me deare indeed," etc.
Respectable people, still liking the name, changed it to Nancy, and in that form it still lives.
Parnel, the once favourite Petronilla, fell under the same blight as Peter, and shared his fate; but her character also ruined her. In the registers of St. Peter, Cornhill, we find the following entries:—
"1539, May 20. Christened Petronilla, ignoti cognominis."
"1594, Sep. 15. Christening of Parnell Griphin, d. of John Griphin, felt-maker."
"1586, April 17. Christening of Parnell Averell, d. of William Averell, merchant tailor."
Two other examples may be furnished:—
"1553, Nov. 15. Peternoll, daughter of William Agar, baptized."—St. Columb Major.
"1590, April. Pernell, d. of Antony Barton, of Poplar."—Stepney, London.
The Restoration did not restore Parnel, and the name is gone.
Sibyl had a tremendous run in her day, and narrowly escaped a second epoch of favour in the second Charles's reign. Tib and Sib were always placed side by side. Burton, speaking of "love melancholy," says—
"One grows too fat, another too lean: modest Matilda, pretty pleasing Peg, sweet singing Susan, mincing merry Moll, dainty dancing Doll, neat Nancy, jolly Joan, nimble Nell, kissing Kate, bouncing Bess with black eyes, fair Phillis with fine white hands, fiddling Frank, tall Tib, slender Sib, will quickly lose their grace, grow fulsome, stale, sad, heavy, dull, sour, and all at last out of fashion."

The "Psalm of Mercie," too, has it:

"'So, so,' quoth my sister Bab,
And 'Kill 'um,' quoth Margerie;
'Spare none,' cry's old Tib; 'No quarter,' says Sib,
'And, hey, for our monachie.'"

In "Cocke Lorelle's Bote," one of the personages introduced is—

"Sibby Sole, mylke wyfe of Islynton."

"Sibb Smith, near Westgate, Canterbury, 1650."—"Half-penny Tokens of Seventeenth Century."

"1590, Aug. 30. Christening of Cibell Overton, d. of Lawrence Overton, bowyer."

Three names practically disappeared in this same century—Olive, Jacomyn or Jacolin, and Grissel:

"1581, Feb. 17. Baptized Olyff, daughter of Degorie Stubbs."—St. Columb Major.

"1550, Dec. 11. Christning of Grysell, daughter of — Plummer."—St. Peter, Cornhill.

"1598, March 15. Buried Jacolyn Backley, widow."—St. Dionis Backchurch.

Olive was a great favourite in the west of England, and was restored by a caprice of fashion as Olivia in the eighteenth century. It was the property of both sexes, and is often found in the dress of "Olliph," "Olyffe," and "Olif." From being a household pet, Dorothy, as Doll, almost disappeared for a while. Doll and Dolly came back in the eighteenth century, under the patronage of the royal and stately Dorothea. What a run it again had! Dolly is one of the few instances of a really double existence. It was the rage from 1450 to 1570; it was overwhelmed with favour from 1750 to 1820. Dr. Syntax in his travels meets with three Dollys. Napoleon is besought in the rhymes of the day to

"quit his folly,
Settle in England, and marry Dolly."

Once more Dolly, saving for Dora, has made her bow and exit. I suppose she may turn up again about 1990, and all the little girls will be wearing Dolly Vardens.

Barbara, with its pet Bab, is now of rarest use. Dowse, the pretty Douce of earlier days, is defunct, and with it the fuller Dowsabel:

"1565, Sep. 9. Buried Dowse, wife of John Thomas."—St. Dionis Backchurch.

Joyce fought hard, but it was useless:

"1563, Sep. 8. Buried Joyce, wife of Thomas Armstrong."—St. Dionis Backchurch.

"1575, April 5. Baptized Joyes, daughter of John Lyttacott."—St. Columb Major.

"1652, Aug. 18. Married Joseph Sumner and Joyce Stallowhace."—St. Peter, Cornhill.

Lettice disappeared, to come back as Lætitia in the eighteenth century:

"1587, June 19. Married Richard Evannes and Lettis Warren."—St. Peter, Cornhill.

Amery, or Emery, the property of either sex, lost place:

"1584, April 9. Buried Amery Martin, widow, of Wilsdon."—St. Peter, Cornhill.

"1668. Emerre Bradley, baker, Hartford."—"Tokens of Seventeenth Century."

Avice shared the same fate:

"Avis Kingston and Amary Clerke, widow, applied for arrears of pay due to their husbands, May 13, 1656."—C. S. P.

"1590-1, Jan. Christened Avis, d. of Philip Cliff."—Stepney.

"1600, Feb. 6. Baptized Avice, daughter of Thomas Bennett."—St. Columb Major.

"1623, August 5. Christened Thomas, the sonne of James Jennets, and Avice his wife."—St. Peter, Cornhill.

Thomasine requires a brief notice. Coming into use as a fancy name about 1450, it seems to have met with no opposition, and for a century and a half was a decided success. It became familiar to every district in England, north or south, and is found in the registers of out-of-the-way villages in Derbyshire, as plentifully as in those of the metropolitan churches:

"1538, Nov. 30. Married Edward Bashe and Thomeson Agar."—St. Dionis Backchurch.

"1582, Nov. 1. Baptized Tamson, daughter of Richard Hodge."—St. Columb Major.

"1622, Jan. 19. Christened Thomas, the sonne of Henery Thomson, haberdasher, and of Thomazine his wife."—St. Peter, Cornhill.

"1620, Jan. 21. Baptized Johanna, fil. Tamsin Smith, adulterina."—Minster.

"1640, Jan. 31. Buried Thomasing, filia William Sympson."—Wirksworth, Derbyshire.

In other registers such forms as Thomasena, Thomesin, Thomazin, Tomasin, and Thomasin occur. In Cowley's "Chronicle," too, the name is found:

"Then Jone and Jane and Audria,

And then a pretty Thomasine,

And then another Katharine,

And then a long et cætera."

V. The General Confusion.

But what a state of confusion does all this reveal! By the time of the Commonwealth, there was the choice of three methods of selection open to the English householder in this matter of names. He might copy the zealot faction, and select his names from the Scriptures or the category of Christian graces; he might rally by the old English gentleman, who at this time was generally a Cavalier, and Dick, Tom, Harry, or Dolly, his children; or he might be careless about the whole matter, and mix the two, according to his caprice or fancy. That Royalist had no bad conception of the state of society in 1648, when he turned off verses such as these:

"And Greenwich shall be for tenements free

For saints to possess Pell-Mell,

And where all the sport is at Hampton Court

Shall be for ourselves to dwell.

Chorus. ''Tis blessed,' quoth Bathsheba,

And Clemence, 'We're all agreed.'

''Tis right,' quoth Gertrude, 'And fit,' says sweet Jude,

And Thomasine, 'Yea, indeed.'

"What though the king proclaims

Our meetings no more shall be;

In private we may hold forth the right way,
And be, as we should be, free.
Chorus. 'O very well said,' quoth Con;
'And so will I do,' says Franck;
And Mercy cries, 'Aye,' and Mat, 'Really,'
'And I'm o' that mind,' quoth Thank."

As we shall show in our next chapter, "Thank" was no imaginary name, coined to meet the exigencies of rhyme. Thanks, however, to the good sense of the nation, an effort was made in behalf of such old favourites as John, William, Richard, Robert, and Thomas. So early as 1643, Thomas Adams, Puritan as he was, had delivered himself in a London pulpit to the effect that "he knew 'Williams' and 'Richards' who, though they bore names not found in sacred story, but familiar to the country, were as gracious saints" as any who bore names found in it ("Meditations upon the Creed"). The Cavalier, we know, had deliberately stuck by the old names. A political skit, already referred to, after running through a list of all the new-fangled names introduced by the fanatics, concludes:

"They're just like the Gadaren's swine,
Which the devils did drive and bewitch:
An herd set on evill
Will run to the de-vill
And his dam when their tailes do itch.
'Then let 'em run on!'
Says Ned, Tom, and John.
'Ay, let 'um be hanged!' quoth Mun:
'They're mine,' quoth old Nick,
'And take 'um,' says Dick,
'And welcome!' quoth worshipful Dun.
'And God blesse King Charles!' quoth George,
'And save him,' says Simon and Sill;
'Aye, aye,' quoth old Cole and each loyall soul,
'And Amen, and Amen!' cries Will."

Another ballad, lively and free as the other, published in 1648, and styled "The Anarchie, or the Blest Reformation," after railing at the confusion of things in general, and names in particular, concludes with the customary jolly old English flourish:

"'A health to King Charles!' says Tom;
'Up with it,' says Ralph like a man;
'God bless him,' says Moll, 'And raise him,' says Doll,
'And send him his owne,' says Nan."

The Restoration practically ended the conflict, but it was a truce; for both sides, so far as nomenclature is concerned, retained trophies of victory, and, on the whole, the Hebrew was the gainer. At the start he had little to lose, and he has filled the land with titles that had lain in abeyance for four thousand years. The old English yeoman has lost many of his most honoured cognomens, but he can still, at least, boast one thing. The two names that were foremost before the middle of the twelfth century stand at this moment in the same position. Out of every hundred children baptized in England, thirteen are entered in the register as John or William. The Cavalier, too, can boast that "Charles," although there were not more of that name throughout the length and breadth of England at the beginning of Elizabeth's reign than could be counted on the fingers of one hand, now occupies the sixth place among male baptismal names.

Several names, now predominant, were for various reasons lifted above the contest. George holds the fourth position among boys; Mary and Elizabeth, the first and second among girls. George dates all his popularity from the last century, and Mary was in danger of becoming obsolete at the close of Elizabeth's reign, so hateful had it become to Englishmen, whether Churchmen or Presbyterians. It was at this time Philip, too, lost a place it can never recover. But the fates came to the rescue of Mary, when the Prince of Orange landed at Torbay, and sate with James's daughter on England's throne. It has been first favourite ever since. As for Elizabeth, a chapter might be written upon it. Just known, and no more, at the beginning of the sixteenth century, it was speedily popularized in the "daughter of the Reformation." The Puritans, in spite of persecution and other provocations, were ever true to "Good Queen Bess." The name, too, was scriptural, and had not been mixed up with centuries of Romish superstition. Elizabeth ruled supreme, and was contorted and twisted into every conceivable shape that ingenuity could devise. It narrowly escaped the diminutive desinence, for Ezot and Ezota occur to my knowledge four times in records between 1500 and 1530. But Bess and Bessie took up the running, and, a century later, Bett and Betty. It will surprise almost all my readers, I suspect, to know that the "Lady Bettys" of the early part of last century were never, or rarely ever, christened Elizabeth. Queen Anne's reign, even William and Mary's reign, saw the fashionable rage for Latinized forms, already referred to, setting in. Elizabeth was turned into Bethia and Betha:

"1707, Jan. 2. Married Willm. Simonds and Bethia Ligbourne."—St. Dionis Backchurch.

"1721. Married Charles Bawden to Bethia Thornton."—Somerset House Chapel.

"1748. Married Adam Allyn to Bethia Lee."—Ditto.

The familiar form of this was Betty:

"Betty Trevor, wife of the Hon. John Trevor, eldest d. of Sir Thomas Frankland, of Thirkleby, in the county of York, Baronet, ob. Dec. 28, 1742, ætat. 25."—"Suss. Arch. Coll.," xvii. 148.

Bess was forgotten, and it was not till the present century that, Betty having become the property of the lower orders, who had soon learnt to copy their betters, the higher classes fell back once more on the Bessie of Reformation days.

Meanwhile other freaks of fancy had a turn. Bessie and Betty were dropped into a mill, and ground out as Betsy. This, after a while, was relegated to the peasantry and artisans north of Trent. Then Tetty and Tetsy had an innings. Dr. Johnson always called his wife Tetty. Writing March 28, 1753, he says—

"I kept this day as the anniversary of my Tetty's death, with prayer and tears in the morning."

Eliza arose before Elizabeth died; was popular in the seventeenth, much resorted to in the eighteenth, and is still familiar in the nineteenth century. Thomas Nash, in "Summer's Last Will and Testament," has the audacity to speak of the queen as—

"that Eliza, England's beauteous queen,

On whom all seasons prosperously attend."

Dr. Johnson, in an epigram anent Colley Cibber and George II., says—

"Augustus still survives in Maro's strain,

And Spenser's verse prolongs Eliza's reign."

But by the lexicographer's day, the poorer classes had ceased to recognize that Eliza and Betty were parts of one single name. They took up each on her own account, as a separate name, and thus Betty and Eliza were commonly met with in the same household. This is still frequently seen. The Spectator, the other day, furnished a list of our commonest font names, wherein Elizabeth is placed fourth, with 4610 representatives in every 100,000 of the population. Looking lower down, we find "Eliza" ranked in the twenty-first place with 1507. This is scarcely fair. The two ought to be added together; at least, it perpetuates a misconception.

CHAPTER II.

PURITAN ECCENTRICITIES.

"And we have known Williams and Richards, names not found in sacred story, but familiar to our country, prove as gracious saints as any Safe-deliverance, Fight-the-good-fight-of-faith, or such like, which have been rather descriptions than names."—Thomas Adams, Meditations upon the Creed, 1629.

"In giving names to children, it was their opinion that heathenish names should be avoided, as not so fit for Christians; and also the names of God, and Christ, and angels, and the peculiar offices of the Mediator,"—Neal, History of the Puritans, vol. 1, ch. v. 1565.

I. Introductory.

There are still many people who are sceptical about the stories told against the Puritans in the matter of name-giving. Of these some are Nonconformists, who do not like the slights thus cast upon their spiritual ancestry; unaware that while this curious phase was at its climax, Puritanism was yet within the pale of the Church of England. Others, having searched through the lists of the Protector's Parliaments, Commissioners, and army officers, and having found but a handful of odd baptismal names, declare, without hesitation, that these stories are wicked calumnies. Mr. Peacock, whose book on the "Army Lists of Roundheads and Cavaliers" is well worth study, says, in one of the numbers of Notes and Queries—

"I know modern writers have repeated the same thing over and over again; but I do not remember any trustworthy evidence of the Commonwealth time, or that of Charles II., that would lead us to believe that strange christian names were more common in those days than now. What passages have we on this subject in the works of the Restoration playwrights?"

This is an old mistake. If Mr. Peacock had looked at our registers from 1580 to 1640, instead of from 1640 to 1680, he would never have written the above. There is the most distinct evidence that during the latter portion of Elizabeth's reign, the whole of James's reign, and great part of Charles's reign, in a district roughly comprising England south of the Trent, and having, say, Banbury for its centre, there prevailed, amongst a certain class of English religionists, a practice of baptizing children by scriptural phrases, pious ejaculations, or godly admonitions. It was a practice instituted of deliberate purpose, as conducive to vital religion, and as intending to separate the truly godly and renewed portion of the community from the world at large. The Reformation epoch had seen the English middle and lower classes generally adopting the proper names of Scripture. Thus, the sterner Puritan had found a list of Bible names that he would gladly have monopolized, shared in by half the English population. That a father should style his child Nehemiah, or Abacuck, or Tabitha, or Dorcas, he discovered with dismay, did not prove that that particular parent was under any deep conviction of sin. This began to trouble the minds and consciences of the elect. Fresh limits must be created. As Richard and Roger had given way to Nathaniel and Zerrubabel, so Nathaniel and Zerrubabel must now give way to Learn-wisdom and Hate-evil. Who inaugurated the movement, with what success, and how it slowly waned, this chapter will show.

There can be no doubt that it is entirely owing to Praise-God Barebone, and the Parliament that went by his name, the impression got abroad in after days that the Commonwealth period was the heyday of these eccentricities, and that these remarkable names were merely adopted after conversion, and were not entered in the vestry-books as baptismal names at all.

The existence of these names could not escape the attention of Lord Macaulay and Sir Walter Scott. The Whig historian has referred to Tribulation Wholesome and Zeal-of-the-land Busy almost as frequently as to that fourth-form boy for whose average (!) abilities to the very end of his literary life he entertained such a profound respect. Two quotations will suffice. In his "Comic Dramatists of the Restoration" he says, speaking of the Commonwealth—

"To know whether a man was really godly was impossible. But it was easy to know whether he had a plain dress, lank hair, no starch in his linen, no gay furniture in his house; whether he talked through his nose, and showed the whites of his eyes; whether he named his children Assurance, Tribulation, and Maher-shalal-hash-baz."

Again, in his Essay on Croker's "Boswell's Life of Johnson," he declares—

"Johnson could easily see that a Roundhead who named all his children after Solomon's singers, and talked in the House of Commons about seeking the Lord, might be an unprincipled villain, whose religious mummeries only aggravated his fault."

In "Woodstock," Scott has such characters as Zerrubabel Robins and Merciful Strickalthrow, both soldiers of Oliver Cromwell; while the zealot ranter is one Nehemiah Holdenough. Mr. Peacock most certainly has grounds for complaint here, but not as to facts, only dates.

II. Originated by the Presbyterian Clergy.

In Strype's "Life of Whitgift" (i. 255) we find the following statement:—

"I find yet again another company of these fault-finders with the Book of Common Prayer, in another diocese, namely, that of Chichester, whose names and livings were these: William Hopkinson, vicar of Salehurst; Samuel Norden, parson of Hamsey; Antony Hobson, vicar of Leominster; Thomas Underdown, parson of St. Mary's in Lewes; John Bingham, preacher of Hodeleigh; Thomas Heley, preacher of Warbleton; John German, vicar of Burienam; and Richard Whiteaker, vicar of Ambreley."

I follow up the history of but two of these ministers, Hopkinson of Salehurst, and Heley of Warbleton. Suspended by the commissary, they were summoned to Canterbury, December 6, 1583, and subscribed. Both being married men, with young families, we may note their action in regard to name-giving. The following are to be found in the register at Salehurst:

"Maye 3, 1579, was baptized Persis (Rom. xvi. 12), the daughter of William Hopkinson, minister heare.

"June 18, 1587, was baptized Stedfast, the sonne of Mr. William Bell, minister.

"Nov. 3, 1588, was baptized Renewed, the daughter of William Hopkinson, minister.

"Feb. 28, 1591, was baptized Safe-on-Highe, the sonne of Willm. Hopkinson, minister of the Lord's Worde there.

"Oct. 29, 1596. Constant, filia Thomæ Lorde, baptisata fuit.

"March, 1621. Rejoyce, filia Thomæ Lorde, baptisata fuit die 10, et sepulta die 23.

"November, 1646. Bethshua, doughter of Mr. John Lorde, minister of Salehurst, bapt. 22 die."

These entries are of the utmost importance; they begin at the very date when the new custom arose, and are patronized by three ministers in succession—possibly four, if Thomas Lorde was also a clergyman.

Heley's case is yet more curious. He had been prescribing grace-names for his flock shortly before the birth of his first child. He thus practises upon his own offspring:

"Nov. 7, 1585. Muche-merceye, the sonne of Thomas Hellye, minyster."

"March 26, 1587. Increased, the dather of Thomas Helly, minister."

"Maye 5, 1588. Sin-denie, the dather of Thomas Helly, minister."

"Maye 25, 1589. Fear-not, the sonne of Thomas Helly, minister."

Under rectorial pressure the villagers followed suit; and for half a century Warbleton was, in the names of its parishioners, a complete exegesis of justification by faith without the deeds of the law. Sorry-for-sin Coupard was a peripatetic exhortation to repentance, and No-merit Vynall was a standing denunciation of works. No register in England is better worth a pilgrimage to-day than Warbleton.

Still confining our attention to Sussex and Kent, we come to Berwick:

"1594, Dec. 22. Baptized Continent, daughter of Hugh Walker, vicar.

"1602, Dec. 12. Baptized Christophilus, son of Hugh Walker."—Berwick, Sussex.

I think the father ought to be whipped most incontinently in the open market who would inflict such a name on an infant daughter. They did not think so then. The point, however, is that the father was incumbent of the parish.

A more historic instance may be given. John Frewen, Puritan rector of Northiam, Sussex, from 1583 to 1628, and author of "Grounds and Principles of the Christian Religion," had two sons, at least, baptized in his church. The dates tally exactly with the new custom:

"1588, May 26. Baptized Accepted, sonne of John Frewen.

"1591, Sep. 5. Baptized Thankful, sonne of John Frewen."—Northiam, Sussex.

Accepted died Archbishop of York, being prebend designate of Canterbury so early as 1620:

"1620, Sep. 8. Grant in reversion to Accepted Frewen of a prebend in Canterbury Cathedral."—"C. S. P. Dom."

One more instance before we pass on. In two separate wills, dated 1602 and 1604 (folio 25, Montagu, "Prerog. Ct. of Cant.," and folio 25, Harte, ditto), will be found references to "More-fruite and Faint-not, children of Dudley Fenner, minister of the Word of God" at Marden, in Kent.

Now, this Dudley Fenner was a thoroughly worthy man, but a fanatic of most intolerant type. In 1583 we find him at Cranbrook, in Kent. An account of his sayings and doings was forwarded, says Strype, to Lord Burghley, who himself marked the following passage:—

"Ye shall pray also that God would strike through the sides of all such as go about to take away from the ministers of the Gospel the liberty which is granted them by the Word of God."

But a curious note occurs alongside this passage in Lord Burghley's hand:

"Names given in baptism by Dudley Fenner: Joy-againe, From-above, More-fruit, Dust."—

Whitgift, i. p. 247.

Two of these names were given to his own children, as Cranbrook register shows to this day:

"1583, Dec. 22. Baptized More-fruit, son of Mr. Dudley Fenner."

"1585, June 6. Baptized Faint-not, fil. Mr. Dudley Fenner, concional digniss."

Soon after this Dudley Fenner again got into trouble through his sturdy spirit of nonconformity. After an imprisonment of twelve months, he fled to Middleborough, in Holland, and died there about 1589.

The above incident from Strype is interesting, for here manifestly is the source whence Camden derived his information upon the subject. In his quaint "Remaines," published thirty years later (1614), after alluding to the Latin names then in vogue, he adds:

"As little will be thought of the new names, Free-Gift, Reformation, Earth, Dust, Ashes, Delivery, More-fruit, Tribulation, The-Lord-is-near, More-triale, Discipline, Joy-againe, From-above, which have lately been given by some to their children, with no evill meaning, but upon some singular and precise conceite."

Very likely Lord Burghley gave Fenner's selection to the great antiquary.

Coming into London, the following case occurs. John Press was incumbent of St. Matthew, Friday Street, from 1573 to 1612:

"1584. Baptized Purifie, son of Mr. John Presse, parson."

John Bunyan's great character name of Hopeful is to be seen in Banbury Church register. But such an eccentricity is to be expected in the parish over which Wheatley presided, the head-quarters, too, of extravagant Puritanism. We all remember drunken Barnaby:

"To Banbury came I, O prophane one!

Where I saw a Puritane one,

Hanging of his cat on Monday

For killing of a mouse on Sunday."

But the point I want to emphasize is that this Hopeful was Wheatley's own daughter:

"1604, Dec. 21. Baptized Hope-full, daughter of William Wheatlye."

Take a run from Banbury into Leicestershire. A stern Puritan was Antony Grey, "parson and patron" of Burbach; and he continued "a constant and faithfull preacher of the Gospell of Jesus Christ, even to his extreame old age, and for some yeares after he was Earle of Kent," as his tombstone tells us. He had twelve children, and their baptismal entries are worth recording:

"1593, April 29. Grace, daughter of Mr. Anthonie Grey.

"1594, Nov. 28. Henry, son of ditto.

"1596, Nov. 16. Magdalen, daughter of ditto.

"1598, May 8. Christian, daughter of ditto.

"1600, Feb. 2. Faith-my-joy, daughter of ditto.

"1603, April 3. John, son of ditto.

"1604, Feb. 23. Patience, daughter of Myster Anthonie Grey, preacher.

"1606, Oct. 5. Jobe, son of ditto.

"1608, May 1. Theophilus, son of ditto.

"1609, March 14. Priscilla, daughter of ditto (died).
"1613, Sept. 19. Nathaniel, son of ditto.
"1615, May 7. Presela, daughter of ditto."

Why old Antony was persuaded of the devil to christen his second child by the ungodly agnomen of Henry, we are not informed. It must have given him many a twinge of conscience afterwards.

Had the Puritan clergy confined these vagaries to their own nurseries, it would not have mattered much. But there can be no doubt they used their influence to bias the minds of godparents and witnesses in the same direction. We have only to pitch upon a minister who came under the archbishop's or Lord Treasurer's notice as disaffected, seek out the church over which he presided, scan the register of baptisms during the years of his incumbency, and a batch of extravagant names will at once be unearthed. In the villages of Sussex and Kent, where the personal influence of the recalcitrant clergy seems to have been greatest, the parochial records teem with them.

Thus was the final stage of fanaticism reached, the year 1580 being as nearly as possible the exact date of its development. Thus were English people being prepared for the influx of a large batch of names which had never been seen before, nor will be again. The purely Biblical names, those that commemorated Bible worthies, swept over the whole country, and left ineffaceable impressions. The second stage of Puritan excess, names that savour of eccentricity and fanaticism combined, scarcely reached England north of Trent, and, for lack of volume, have left but the faintest traces. They lasted long enough to cover what may be fairly called an epoch, and extended just far enough to embrace a province. The epoch was a hundred years, and the province was from Kent to Hereford, making a small arc northwards, so as to take in Bedfordshire, Leicestershire, Buckinghamshire, and Oxfordshire. The practice, so far as the bolder examples is concerned, was a deliberate scheme on the part of the Presbyterian clergy. On this point the evidence is in all respects conclusive.

III. Curious Names not Puritan.

Several names found in the registers at this time, though commonly ascribed to the zealots, must be placed under a different category. For instance, original sin and the Ninth Article would seem to be commemorated in such a name as Original. We may reject Camden's theory:

"Originall may seem to be deducted from the Greek origines, that is, borne in good time,"

inasmuch as he does not appear to have believed in it himself. The name, as a matter of fact, was given in the early part of the sixteenth century, in certain families of position, to the eldest son and heir, denoting that in him was carried on the original stock. The Bellamys of Lambcote Grange, Stainton, are a case in point. The eldest son for three generations bore the name; viz. Original Bellamy, buried at Stainton, September 12, 1619, aged 80; Original, his son and heir, the record of whose death I cannot find; and Original, his son and heir, who was baptized December 29, 1606. The first of these must have been born in 1539, far too early a date for the name to be fathered upon the Puritans. Original was in use in the family of Babington, of Rampton. Original Babington, son and heir of John Babington, was a contemporary of the first

Original Bellamy (Nicholl's "Gen. et Top.," viii.).

Another instance occurs later on:

"1635, May 21. These under-written names are to be transported to St. Christopher's, imbarqued in the Matthew of London, Richard Goodladd, master, per warrant from ye Earle of Carlisle:

"Originall Lowis, 28 yeres," etc.—Hotten's "Emigrants," p. 81.

Sense, a common name in Elizabeth and James's reigns, looks closely connected with some of the abstract virtues, such as Prudence and Temperance. The learned compiler of the "Calendar of State Papers" (1637-38) seems to have been much bothered with the name:

"1638, April 23. Petition of Seuce Whitley, widow of Thomas Whitley, citizen, and grocer."

The suggestion from the editorial pen is that this Seuce (as he prints it) is a bewildered spelling of Susey, from Susan! The fact is, Seuce is a bewildered misreading on the compiler's part of Sense, and Sense is an English dress of the foreign Senchia, or Sancho, still familiar to us in Sancho Panza. Several of the following entries will prove that Sense was too early an inmate of our registers to be a Puritan agnomen:

"1564, Oct. 15. Baptized Saints, d. of Francis Muschamp."

"1565, Nov. 25. Buried Sence, d. of ditto."

"1559, June 13. Married Matthew Draper and Sence Blackwell."

"1570-1, Jan. 15. Baptized Sence, d. of John Bowyer."—Camberwell Church.

"1651. Zanchy Harvyn, Grocer's Arms, Abbey Milton."—"Tokens of Seventeenth Century."

"1661, June. Petition of Mrs. Zanchy Mark."—C. S. P.

That it was familiar to Camden in 1614 is clear:

"Sanchia, from Sancta, that is, Holy."—"Remaines," p. 88.

The name became obsolete by the close of the seventeenth century, and, being a saintly title, was sufficiently odious to the Presbyterians to be carefully rejected by them in the sixteenth century. Men who refused the Apostles their saintly title were not likely to stamp the same for life on weak flesh.

Nor can Emanuel, or Angel, be brought as charges against the Puritans. Both flatly contradicted Cartwright's canon; yet both, and especially the former, have been attributed to the zealots. No names could have been more offensive to them than these. Even Adams, in his "Meditations upon the Creed," while attacking his friends on their eccentricity in preferring "Safe-deliverance" to "Richard," takes care to rebuke those on the other side, who would introduce Emanuel, or even Gabriel or Michael, into their nurseries:

"Some call their sons Emanuel: this is too bold. The name is proper to Christ, therefore not to be communicated to any creature."

Emanuel was imported from the Continent about 1500:

"1545, March 19. Baptized Humphrey, son of Emanuell Roger."—St. Columb Major.

The same conclusion must be drawn regarding Angel. Adams continues:

"Yea, it seems to me not fit for Christian humility to call a man Gabriel or Michael, giving the names of angels to the sons of mortality."

If the Puritans objected, as they did to a man, to the use of Gabriel and Michael as angelic names, the generic term itself would be still more objectionable:

"1645, Nov. 13. Buried Miss Angela Boyce."—Cant. Cath.

"1682, April 11. Baptized Angel, d. of Sir Nicholas Butler, Knt."—St. Helen, Bishopgate.

"Weymouth, March 20, 1635. Embarked for New England: Angell Holland, aged 21 years."—Hotten's "Emigrants," p. 285.

In this case we may presume the son, and not the father, had turned Puritan.

A curious custom, which terminated soon after Protestantism was established in England, gave rise to several names which read oddly enough to modern eyes. These were titles like Vitalis or Creature—names applicable to either sex. Mr. Maskell, without furnishing instances, says Creature occurs in the registers of All-Hallows, Barking ("Hist. All-Hallows," p. 62). In the vestry-books of Staplehurst, Kent, are registered:

"1 Edward VI. Apryle xxvii., there were borne ii. childre of Alex'nder Beeryl: the one christened at home, and so deceased, called Creature; the other christened at church, called John."—Burns, "History of Parish Registers," p. 81.

"1550, Nov. 5. Buried Creature, daughter of Agnes Mathews, syngle woman, the seconde childe.

"1579, July 19. Married John Haffynden and Creature Cheseman, yong folke."—Staplehurst, Kent.

One instance of Vitalis may be given:

"Vitalis, son of Richard Engaine, and Sara his wife, released his manor of Dagworth in 1217 to Margery de Cressi."—Blomefield's "Norfolk," vi. 382, 383.

These are not Puritan names. The dates are against the theory. They belong to a pre-Reformation practice, being names given to quick children before birth, in cases when it was feared, from the condition of the mother, they might not be delivered alive. Being christened before the sex could be known, it was necessary to affix a neutral name, and Vitalis or Creature answered the purpose. The old Romish rubric ran thus:

"Nemo in utero matris clausus baptizari debet, sed si infans caput emiserit, et periculum mortis immineat, baptizetur in capite, nec postea si vivus evaserit, erit iterum baptizandus. At si aliud membrum emiserit, quod vitalem indicet motum in illo, si periculum pendeat baptizetur," etc.

Vitalis Engaine and Creature Cheseman, in the above instances, both lived, but, by the law just quoted, retained the names given to them, and underwent no second baptism. If the sex of the yet breathing child was discovered, but death certain, the name of baptism ran thus:

"1563, July 17. Baptizata fuit in ædibus Mri Humfrey filia ejus quæ nominata fuit Creatura Christi."—St. Peter in the East, Oxford.

"1563, July 17. Creatura Christi, filia Laurentii Humfredi sepulta."—Ditto.

An English form occurs earlier:

"1561, June 30. The Chylde-of-God, filius Ric. Stacey."—Ditto.

Without entering into controversy, I will only say that if the clergy, up to the time of the alteration in our Article on Baptism, truly believed that "insomuch as infants, and children dying in their infancy, shall undoubtedly be saved thereby (i.e. baptism), and else not," it was natural that such a delicate ceremonial as I have hinted at should have suggested itself to their minds. After the Reformation, the practice as to unborn children fell into desuetude, and the names with it.

IV. Instances.

(a.) Latin Names.

The elder Disraeli reminded us, in his "Curiosities of Literature," that in the fifteenth and sixteenth centuries it was common for our more learned pundits to re-style themselves in their own studies by Greek and Latin names. Some of these—as, for instance, Erasmus and Melancthon—are only known to the world at large by their adopted titles.

The Reformation had not become an accomplished fact before this custom began to prevail in England, only it was transferred from the study to the font, and from scholars to babies. Renovata, Renatus, Donatus, and Beata began to grow common. Camden, writing in 1614, speaks of still stranger names—

"If that any among us have named their children Remedium, Amoris, 'Imago-sæculi,' or with such-like names, I know some will think it more than a vanity."—"Remaines," p. 44.

While, however, the Presbyterian clergy did not object to some of these Latin sobriquets, as being identical with the names of early believers of the Primitive Church, stamped in not a few instances with the honours of martyrdom, they preferred to translate them into English. Many of my examples of eccentricity will be found to be nothing more than literal translations of names that had been in common vogue among Christians twelve and thirteen hundred years before. To the majority of the Puritan clergy, to change the Latin dress for an English equivalent would be as natural and imperative as the adoption of Tyndale's or the Genevan Bible in the place of the Latin Vulgate.

A curious, though somewhat later, proof of this statement is met with in a will from the Probate Court of Peterborough. The testator was one Theodore Closland, senior fellow of Trinity College, Cambridge. The date is June 24, 1665:

"Item: to What-God-will Crosland, forty shillings, and tenn shillings to his wife. And to his sonne What-God-will, six pound, thirteen shillings, fourpence."

This is a manifest translation of the early Christian "Quod-vult-deus." Grainger, in his "History of England" (iii. 360, fifth edition), says—

"In Montfaucon's 'Diarium Italicum' (p. 270), is a sepulchral inscription of the year 396, upon Quod-vult-deus, a Christian, to which is a note: 'Hoc ævo non pauci erant qui piis sententiolis nomina propria concinnarent, v.g. Quod-vult-deus, Deogratias, Habet-deum, Adeodatus.'"

Closland, or Crosland, the grandfather, was evidently a Puritan, with a horror of the Latin Vulgate, Latin Pope, and Latin everything. Hence the translation.

Nevertheless, the Puritans seem to have favoured Latin names at first. It was a break between the familiar sound of the old and the oddity of the new. Redemptus was less grotesque than Redeemed, and Renata than Renewed. The English equivalents soon ruled supreme, but for a generation or two, and in some cases for a century, the Latin names went side by side with them.

Take Renatus, for instance:

"1616, Sep. 29. Baptized Renatus, son of Renatus Byllett, gent."—St. Columb Major.

"1637-8, Jan. 12. Order of Council to Renatus Edwards, girdler, to shut up his shop in Lombard Street, because he is not a goldsmith.

"1690, April 10. Petition of Renatus Palmer, who prays to be appointed surveyor in the port of Dartmouth."—C. S. P.

"1659, Nov. 11. Baptized Renovata, the daughter of John Durance."—Cant. Cath.

It was Renatus Harris who built the organ in All-Hallows, Barking, in 1675 ("Hist. All-Hallows, Barking," Maskell). Renatus and Rediviva occur in St. Matthew, Friday Street, circa 1590. Rediviva lingered into the eighteenth century:

"1735, ——. Buried Rediviva Mathews."—Banbury.

Desiderata and Desiderius were being used at the close of Elizabeth's reign, and survived the restoration of Charles II.:

"1671, May 26. Baptized Desiderius Dionys, a poor child found in Lyme Street."—St. Dionis Backchurch.

Donatus and Deodatus, also, were Latin names on English soil before the seventeenth century came in:

"1616, Jan. 29. Baptized Donate, vel Deonata, daughter of Martyn Donnacombe."—St. Columb Major.

Desire and Given, the equivalents, both crossed the Atlantic with the Pilgrim Fathers.

Love was popular. Side by side with it went Amor. George Fox, in his "Journal," writing in 1670, says—

"When I was come to Enfield, I went first to visit Amor Stoddart, who lay very weak and almost speechless. Within a few days Amor died."—Ed. 1836, ii. 129.

In Ripon Cathedral may be seen:

"Amor Oxley, died Nov. 23, 1773, aged 74."

The name still exists in Yorkshire, but no other county, I imagine.

Other instances could be mentioned. I place a few in order:

"1594, Aug. 3. Baptized Relictus Dunstane, a childe found in this parisshe."—St. Dunstan.

"1613, Nov. 7. Baptized Beata, d. of Mr. John Briggs, minister."—Witherley, Leic.

"1653, Sep. 29. Married Richard Moone to Benedicta Rolfe."—Cant. Cath.

"1661, May 25. Married Edward Clayton and Melior Billinge."—St. Dionis, Backchurch.

"1706. Beata Meetkirke, born Nov. 2, 1705; died Sep. 10, 1706."—Rushden, Hereford.

(b.) Grace Names.

In furnishing instances, we naturally begin with those grace names, in all cases culled from the registers of the period, which belong to what we may style the first stage. They were, one by one, but taken from the lists found in the New Testament, and were probably suggested at the outset by the moralities or interludes. The morality went between the old miracle-play, or mystery, and the regular drama. In "Every Man," written in the reign of Henry VIII., it is made a vehicle for retaining the love of the people for the old ways, the old worship, and the old superstitions. From the time of Edward VI. to the middle of Elizabeth's reign, there issued a cluster of interludes of this same moral type and cast; only all breathed of the new religion, and more or less assaulted the dogmas of Rome.

These moralities were popular, and were frequently rendered in public, until the Elizabethan drama was well established. All were allegorical, and required personal representatives of the abstract graces, and doctrines of which they treated. The dramatis personæ in "Hickscorner" are Freewill, Perseverance, Pity, Contemplation, and Imagination, and in "The Interlude of Youth," Humility, Pride, Charity, and Lechery.

It is just possible, therefore, that several of these grace names were originated under the shadow of the pre-Reformation Church. The following are early, considering they are found in Cornwall, the county most likely to be the last to take up a new custom:

"1549, July 1. Baptized Patience, d. of Willm. Haygar."—

"1553, May 29. Baptized Honour, d. of Robert Sexton."—St. Columb Major.

However this may be, we only find the cardinal virtues at the beginning of the movement—those which are popular in some places to this day, and still maintain a firm hold in America, borne thither by the Puritan emigrants.

The three Graces, and Grace itself, took root almost immediately as favourites. Shakespeare seems to have been aware of it, for Hermione says—

"My last good deed was to entreat his stay:

What was my first? It has an elder sister,

Or I mistake you—O would her name were Grace!"

"Winter's Tale," Act i. sc. 2.

"1565, March 19. Christening of Grace, daughter of — Hilles."—St. Peter, Cornhill.

"1574, Jan. 29. Baptized Grace, daughter of John Russell."—St. Columb Major.

"1588, Aug. 1. Married Thomas Wood and Faythe Wilson."—St. Dionis Backchurch.

"1565, ——. Baptized Faith, daughter of Thomas and Agnes Blomefield."—Rushall, Norfolk.

"1567, April 17. Christening of Charity, daughter of Randoll Burchenshaw."—St. Peter, Cornhill.

"1571, ——. Baptized Charity, daughter of Thomas Blomefield."—Rushall, Norfolk.

"1598, Nov. 19. Baptized Hope, d. of John Mainwaringe."—Cant. Cath.

"1636, Nov. 25. Buried Hope, d. of Thomas Alford, aged 23."—Drayton, Leicester.

The registers of the sixteenth and seventeenth century teem with these; sometimes boys received them. The Rev. Hope Sherhard was a minister in Providence Isle in 1632 ("Cal. S. P. Colonial," 1632).

We may note that the still common custom of christening trine-born children by these names dates from the period of their rise:

"1639, Sep. 7. Baptized Faith, Hope, and Charity, daughters of George Lamb, and Alice his wife."—Hillingdon.

"1666, Feb. 22. — Finch, wife of — Finch, being delivered of three children, two of them were baptized, one called Faith, and the other Hope; and the third was intended to be called Charity, but died unbaptized."—Cranford. Vide Lyson's "Middlesex," p. 30.

Mr. Lower says ("Essays on English Surnames," ii. 159)—

"At Charlton, Kent, three female children produced at one birth received the names of Faith, Hope, and Charity."

Thomas Adams, in his sermon on the "Three Divine Sisters," says—

"They shall not want prosperity,

That keep faith, hope, and charity."

Perhaps some of these parents remembered this.

Faith and Charity are both mentioned as distinctly Puritan sobriquets in the "Psalm of Mercie," a political poem:

"'A match,' quoth my sister Joyce,

'Contented,' quoth Rachel, too:

Quoth Abigaile, 'Yea,' and Faith, 'Verily,'

And Charity, 'Let it be so.'"

Love, as the synonym of Charity, was also a favourite. Love Atkinson went out to Virginia with the early refugees (Hotten, "Emigrants," p. 68).

"1631-2, Jan. 31. Buried Love, daughter of William Ballard."—Berwick, Sussex.

"1740, April 30. Buried Love Arundell."—Racton, Sussex.

"1749, May 31. Love Luckett admitted a freeman by birthright."—"History of Town and Port of Rye," p. 237.

"1662, May 7. Baptized Love, d. of Mr. Richard Appletree."—Banbury.

Besides Love and Charity, other variations were Humanity and Clemency:

"1637, March 8. Bond of William Shaw, junior, and Thomas Snelling, citizens and turners, to Humanity Mayo, of St. Martin-in-the-Fields, in £100 0 0."—C. S. P.

"1625, Aug. 27. Buried Clemency Chawncey."—St. Dionis Backchurch.

Clemency was pretty, and deserved to live; but Mercy seems to have monopolized the honours, and, by the aid of John Bunyan's heroine in the "Pilgrim's Progress," still has her admirers. Instances are needless, but I furnish one or two for form's sake. They shall be late ones:

"1702, Sep. 28. Married Matthias Wallraven and Mercy Waymarke."—St. Dionis Backchurch.

"1716, May 25. Married Thomas Day and Mercy Parsons, of Staplehurst."—Cant. Cath.

But there were plenty of virtues left. Prudence had such a run, that she became Pru in the sixteenth, and Prudentia in the seventeenth century:

"1574, June 30. Buried Prudence, d. of John Mayhew.

"1612, Aug. 2. Married Robert Browne and Prudence Coxe."—St. Dionis Backchurch.

Justice is hard to separate from the legal title; but here is an instance:

"1660, July 16. Richard Bickley and Justice Willington reported guilty of embezzling late king's goods."—"Cal. St. P. Dom."

Truth, Constancy, Honour, and Temperance were frequently personified at the font. Temperance had the shortest life; but, if short, it was merry. There is scarcely a register, from Gretna Green to St. Michael's, without it:

"1615, Feb. 25. Baptized Temperance, d. of — Osberne."—Hawnes, Bedford.

"1610, Aug. 14. Baptized Temperance, d. of John Goodyer."—Banbury.

"1611, Nov. —. Baptized Temperance, d. of Robert Carpinter."—Stepney.

"1619, July 22. Married Gyles Rolles to Temperance Blinco."—St. Peter, Cornhill.

Constance, Constancy, and Constant were common, it will be seen, to both sexes:

"1593, Sep. 29. Buried Constancy, servant with Mr. Coussin."—St. Dionis Backchurch.

"1629, Dec. Petition of Captain Constance Ferrar, for losses at Cape Breton."—"C. S. P. Colonial."

"1665, May 25. Communication from Constance Pley to the Commissioners in relation to the arrival of a convoy."—C. S. P.

"1665, May 31. Grant to Edward Halshall of £225 0 0, forfeited by Connistant Cant, of Lynn Regis, for embarking wool to Guernsey not entered in the Custom House."—Ditto.

"1671, Sep. 2. Buried Constant Sylvester, Esquire."—Brampton, Hunts.

Patience, too, was male as well as female. Sir Patience Warde was Lord Mayor of London in 1681. Thus the weaker vessels were not allowed to monopolize the graces. How familiar some of these abstract names had become, the Cavalier shall tell us in his parody of the sanctimonious Roundheads' style:

"'Ay, marry,' quoth Agatha,
And Temperance, eke, also:
Quoth Hannah, 'It's just,' and Mary, 'It must,'
'And shall be,' quoth Grace, 'I trow.'"

Several "Truths" occur in the "Chancery Suits" of Elizabeth, and the Greek Alathea arose with it:

"1595, June 27. Faith and Truth, gemini, — John Johnson, bapt."—Wath, Ripon.

Alathea lasted till the eighteenth century was well-nigh out:

"1701, Dec. 4. Francis Milles to Alathea Wilton."—West. Abbey.

"1720, Sep. 18. Buried Alydea, wife of Willm. Gough, aged 42 years."—Harnhill, Glouc.

"1786, Oct. 6. Died Althea, wife of Thomas Heberden, prebendary."—Exeter Cath.

Honour, of course, became Honora, in the eighteenth century, and has retained that form:

"1583, Aug. 24. Baptized Honor, daughter of Thomas Teage."—St. Columb Major.

"1614, July 4. Baptized Honour, d. of John Baylye, of Radcliffe."—Stepney.

"1667, Oct. 9. Christened Mary, d. of Sir John and Lady Honour Huxley."—Hammersmith.

"1722, Oct. 4. Christened Martha, d. of John and Honoria Hart."—St. Dionis Backchurch.

Sir Thomas Carew, Speaker of the Commons in James's and Charles's reign, had a wife Temperance, and four daughters, Patience, Temperance, Silence, and Prudence (Lodge's "Illust.," iii. 37). Possibly, as Speaker, he had had better opportunity to observe that these were the four cardinal parliamentary virtues, especially Silence. This last was somewhat popular, and seems to have got curtailed to "Sill," as Prudence to "Pru," and Constance to "Con." In the Calendar of "State Papers" (June 21, 1666), a man named Taylor, writing to another named Williamson, wishes "his brother Sill would come and reap the sweets of Harwich." Writing again, five days later, he asks "after his brother, Silence Taylor."

This was one of the names that crossed the Atlantic and became a fixture in America (Bowditch). It is not, however, to be confounded with Sill, that is, Sybil, in the old Cavalier chorus:

"'And God blesse King Charles,' quoth George,
'And save him,' says Simon and Sill."

Silence is one of the few Puritan names that found its way into the north of England:

"1741, Dec. 9. Married Robert Thyer to Silence Leigh."—St. Ann, Manchester.

The mother of Silence Leigh, who was a widow when she married, was Silence Beswicke ("Memorials of St. Ann, Manchester," p. 55). The name is found again in the register of Youlgreave Church, Derbyshire (Notes and Queries, Feb. 17, 1877). Curiously enough, we find Camden omitting Silence as a female name of his day, but inserting Tace. In his list of feminine baptismal names, compiled in 1614 ("Remaines," p. 89), he has

"Tace—Be silent—a fit name to admonish that sex of silence."

Here, then, is another instance of a Latin name translated into English. I have lighted on a case proving the antiquary's veracity:

"Here lieth the body of Tacey, the wife of George Can, of Brockwear, who departed this life 22 day of Feb., An. Dom. 1715, aged 32 years."—Hewelsfield, Glouc.

Tace must have lasted a century, therefore. Silence may be set down to some old Puritan stickler for the admonition of Saint Paul: "Let the woman learn in silence, with all subjection" (1 Tim. ii. 11).

The Epistle to the Romans was a never-failing well-spring to the earnest Puritan, and one passage was much applied to his present condition:

"Therefore being justified by faith, we have peace with God through our Lord Jesus Christ: by whom also we have access by faith unto this grace wherein we stand, and rejoice in hope of the glory of God. And not only so, but we glory in tribulations also: knowing that tribulation worketh patience; and patience, experience; and experience, hope: and hope maketh not ashamed."—v. 1-5.

There is scarcely a word in this passage that is not inscribed on our registers between 1575 and 1595. Faith, Grace, and Hope have already been mentioned; Camden testified to the existence of Tribulation in 1614; Rejoice was very familiar; Patience, of course, was common:

"1592, July 7. Buried Patience Birche."—Cant. Cath.

"1596, Oct. 3. Baptized Pacience, daughter of Martin Tome."—St. Columb Major.

"1599, April 23. Baptized Patience, d. of John Harmer."—Warbleton.

Even Experience is found—a strange title for an infant.

"The Rev. Experience Mayhew, A.M., born Feb. 5, 1673; died of an apoplexy, Nov. 9, 1758."

So ran the epitaph of a missionary (vide Pulpit, Dec. 6, 1827) to the Vineyard Island. It had been handed on to him, no doubt, from some grandfather or grandmother of Elizabeth's closing days.

A late instance of Diligence occurs in St. Peter, Cornhill:

"1724, Nov. 1. Buried Diligence Constant."

Obedience had a good run, and began very early:

"1573, Sep. 20. Bapt. Obedience, dather of Thomas Garding."

"1586, Aug. 28. Bapt. Obedyence, dather of Richard Ellis."—Warbleton.

"1697, April 30. Bapt. Robert, son of James and Obedience Clark."—St. James, Picadilly.

Obedience Robins is the name of a testator in 1709 (Wills: Archdeaconry of London), while the following epitaph speaks for itself:

"Obedience Newitt, wife of Thomas Newitt, died in 1617, aged 32.

"Her name and nature did accord,

Obedient was she to her Lord."—Burwash, Sussex.

"Add to your faith, virtue," says the Apostle. As a name this grace was late in the field:

"1687, May 25. Married Virtue Radford and Susannah Wright."—West. Abbey.

"1704, Oct. 20. Buried Virtue, wife of John Higgison."—Marshfield, Glouc.

"1709, May 6. Buried Vertue Page."—Finchley.

Confidence and Victory were evidently favourites:

"1587, Jan. 8. Baptized Confydence, d. of Roger Elliard."—Warbleton.

"1770, Nov. 17, died Confidence, wife of John Thomas, aged 61 years."—Bulley, Glouc.

"1587, Feb. 8. Buryed Vyctorye Buttres."—Elham, Kent.

"1618, Dec. 9. Buryed Victorye Lussendine."—Ditto.

"1696, May 17. Bapt. Victory, d. of Joseph Gibbs."—St. Dionis Backchurch.

Perseverance went out with the emigrants to New England, but I do not find any instance in the home registers. Felicity appeared in one of our law courts last year, so it cannot be said to be extinct; but there is a touch of irony in the first of the following examples:—

"1604-5, March 15. Baptized Felicity, d. of John Barnes, vagarant."—Stepney.

"1590, July 5. Baptized Felycyte Harris."—Cranbrook.

Comfort has a pleasant atmosphere about it, and many a parent was tempted to the use of it. It lingered longer than many of its rivals. Comfort Farren's epitaph may be seen on the floor of Tewkesbury Abbey:

"Comfort, wife of Abraham Farren, gent., of this Corporation, died August 24, 1720."

Again, in Dymock Church we find:

"Comfort, wife to William Davis, died 14 June, 1775, aged 78 years.

"Comfort, their daughter, died 9 Feb., 1760, aged 24 years."

Nearly 150 years before this, however, Comfort Starr was a name not unknown to the more heated zealots of the Puritan party. He was a native of Ashford, in Kent, and after various restless shiftings as a minister, Carlisle being his head-quarters for a time, went to New Plymouth in the Mayflower, in 1620. There he became fellow of Harvard College, but returned to England eventually, and died at Lewes in his eighty-seventh year.

Perhaps the most interesting and popular of the grace names was "Repentance." In a "new interlude" of the Reformation, entitled the "Life and Repentance of Marie Magdalene," and published in 1567, one of the chief characters was "Repentance." At the same time Repentance came into font use, and, odd as it may sound, bade fair to become a permanently recognized name in England:

"1583, Dec. 8. Married William Arnolde and Repentance Pownoll."—Cant. Cath.

"1587, Oct. 22. Baptized Repentance, dather of George Aysherst."—Warbleton.

"1588, June 30. Baptized Repentance Water."—Cranbrook.

"1597, Aug. 4. Baptized Repentance, daughter of Robert Benham, of Lymhouse."—Stepney.

"1612, March 26. Baptized Repentance Wrathe."—Elham, Kent.

"1688, Dec. 23. Bapt. Repentance, son of Thomas and Mercy Tompson."—St. James, Piccadilly.

In the "Sussex Archæological Collections" (xvii. 148) is found recorded the case of Repentance Hastings, deputy portreeve of Seaford, who in 1643 was convicted of hiding some wreckage:

"Repentance Hastings, 1 load, 1 cask, 2 pieces of royals."

Evidently his repentance began too early in life to be lasting; but infant piety could not be expected to resist the hardening influence of such a name as this.

Humiliation was a big word, and that alone must have been in its favour:

"1629, Jan. 24. Married Humiliation Hinde and Elizabeth Phillips by banes."—St. Peter, Cornhill.

Humiliation, being proud of his name, determined to retain it in the family—for he had one—but as he had began to worship at St. Dionis Backchurch, the entries of baptism lie there, the spelling of his surname being slightly altered:

"1630, Nov. 18. Baptized Humiliation, son of Humiliation Hyne."

This son died March 11, 1631-2. Humiliation père, however, did not sorrow without hope, for in a few years he again brings a son to the parson:

"1637-8, Jan. 21. Baptized Humiliation, son of Humiliation Hinde."

Humility is preferable to Humiliation. Humility Cooper was one of a freight of passengers in the Mayflower, who, in 1620, sought a home in the West. A few years afterwards Humility Hobbs followed him (Hotten, "Emigrants," p. 426):

"1596, March 13. Baptized Humilitye, sonne of Wylliam Jones."—Warbleton.

"1688, May 5. Buried Humility, wife of Humphey Paget."—Peckleton, Leic.

Had it not been for Charles Dickens, Humble would not have appeared objectionable:

"1666-1667, Jan. 29. Petition of Dame Frances, wife of Humble Ward, Lord Ward, Baron, of Birmingham."—C. S. P.

All Saints, Leicester, records another saintly grace:

"Here lieth the body of Abstinence Pougher, Esq., who died Sept. 5, 1741, aged 62 years."

In some cases we find the infant represented, not by a grace-name, but as in a state of grace. Every register contains one or two Godlies:

"1579, July 24. Baptized Godlye, d. of Richard Fauterell."—Warbleton.

"1611, May 1. Baptized Godly, d. of Henry Gray, and Joane his wife. Joane Standmer and Godly Gotherd, sureties."—South Bersted, Sussex.

"1619, Nov. Baptized Godly, d. of Thomas Edwardes, of Poplar."—Stepney.

"1632, Oct. 30. Married John Wafforde to Godly Spicer."—Cant. Cath.

Gracious is as objectionable as Godly. Gracious Owen was President of St. John's College, Oxford, during the decade 1650-1660.

"Oct. 24, 1661. Examination of Gracious Franklin: Joshua Jones, minister at the Red Lion, Fleet Street, told him that he heard there were 3000 men about the city maintained by Presbyterian ministers."—C. S. P.

Lively, we may presume, referred to spiritual manifestations. A curious combination of font name and patronymic is obtained in Lively Moody, D.D., of St. John's College, Cambridge, 1682 (Wood's "Fasti Oxonienses"). Exactly one hundred years later the name is met with again:

"1782, July 3. Lively Clarke of this town, sadler, aged 60."—Berkeley, Gloucester.

At Warbleton, where the Puritan Heley ministered, it seems to have been found wearisome to be continually christening children by the names of Repent and Repentance, so a variation was made in the form of "Sorry-for-sin:"

"1589, Jan 25. Baptized Sory-for-sine, the dather of John Coupard."

The following is curious:

"Thomas Luxford, of Windmill Hill, died Feb. 24, 1739, aged 72 years. He was grandson of Thomas Luxford, of Windmill Hill, by Changed Collins, his wife, daughter of Thomas Collins, of Socknash in this county, Esq., and eldest son of Richard Luxford, of Billinghurst."—Wartling Church.

Faithful may close this list:

"1640, Oct. 18. Baptized Benjamin, son of Faithful Bishop."—St. Columb Major.

Faithful Rouse settled in New England in 1644 (Bowditch). The following despatch mentions another:

"1666, July 18. Major Beversham and Lieut. Faithful Fortescue are sent from Ireland to raise men."—C. S. P.

Bunyan evidently liked it, and gave the name to the martyr of Vanity Fair:

"Sing, Faithful, sing, and let thy name survive;

For though they killed thee, thou art yet alive."

Speaking from a nomenclatural point of view, the name did not survive, for the last instance I have met with is that of Faithful Meakin, curate of Mobberley, Cheshire, in 1729 (Earwaker, "East Cheshire," p. 99, n.). It had had a run of more than a century, however.

The reader will have observed that the majority of these names have become obsolete. The religious apathy of the early eighteenth century was against them. They seem to have made their way slowly westward. Certainly their latest representatives are to be found in the more retired villages of Gloucestershire and Devonshire. A few like Mercy, Faith, Hope, Charity, Grace, and Prudence, still survive, and will probably for ever command a certain amount of patronage; but they are much more popular in our religious story-books than the church registers. The absence of the rest is no great loss, I imagine.

(c.) Exhortatory Names.

The zealots of Elizabeth's later days began to weary of names that merely made household words of the apostolic virtues. Many of these sobriquets had become popular among the unthinking and careless. They began to stamp their offspring with exhortatory sentences, pious ejaculations, brief professions of godly sorrow for sin, or exclamations of praise for mercies received. I am bound to confess, however, that the prevailing tone of these names is rather contradictory of the picture of gloomy sourness drawn by the facile pens of Macaulay and Walter Scott. 'Tis true, Anger and Wrath existed:

"1654. Wroth Rogers to be placed on the Commission of Scandalous Ministers."—Scobell's "Acts and Ord. Parl.," 1658.

"1680, Dec. 22. Buried Anger Bull, packer."—St. Dionis Backchurch.

I dare say he was familiarly termed Angry Bull, like "Savage Bear," a gentleman of Kent who was living at the same time, mentioned elsewhere in these pages. Nevertheless, in the exhortatory names there is a general air of cheerful assurance.

The most celebrated name of this class is Praise-God Barebone. I cannot find his baptismal entry. A collection of verses was compiled by one Fear-God Barbon, of Daventry (Harleian M.S. 7332). This cannot have been his father, as we have evidence that the leatherseller was born about 1596, and, allowing his parent to be anything over twenty, the date would be too early for exhortatory names like Fear-God. We may presume, therefore, he was a brother. Two other brothers are said to have been entitled respectively, "Jesus-Christ-came-into-the-world-to-save Barebone," and "If-Christ-had-not-died-for-thee-thou-hadst-been-damned Barebone." I say "entitled," for I doubt whether either received such a long string of words in baptism. Brook, in his "History of the Puritans," implies they were; Hume says that both were adopted names, and adds, in regard to the latter, that his acquaintance were so wearied with its length, that they styled him by the last word as "Damned Barebone." The editor of Notes and Queries (March 15, 1862) says that, "as his morals were not of the best," this abbreviated form "appeared to suit him better than his entire baptismal prefix." Whether the title was given at the font or adopted, there is no doubt that he was familiarly known as Dr. Damned Barebone. This was more curt than courteous.

Of Praise-God's history little items have leaked out. He began life as a leatherseller in Fleet Street, and owned a house under the sign of the "Lock and Key," in the parish of St. Dunstan-in-the-West. He was admitted a freeman of the Leathersellers' Company, January 20, 1623. He was a Fifth Monarchy man, if a tract printed in 1654, entitled "A Declaration of several of the Churches of Christ, and Godly People, in and about the City of London," etc., which mentions "the Church which walks with Mr. Barebone," refers to him. This, however, may be Fear-God Barebone. Praise-God was imprisoned after the Restoration, but after a while released, and died, at the age of eighty or above, in obscurity. His life, which was not without its excitements, was spent in London, and possibly his baptismal entry will be found there.

A word or two about his surname. The elder Disraeli says ("Curiosities of Literature")—

"There are unfortunate names, which are very injurious to the cause in which they are engaged; for instance, the long Parliament in Cromwell's time, called by derision the Rump, was headed by one Barebones, a leatherseller."

Isaac Disraeli has here perpetuated a mistake. Barebone's Parliament was the Parliament of Barebone, not Barebones. Peck, in his "Desiderata Curiosa," speaking of a member of the family who died in 1646, styles him Mr. Barborne; while Echard writes the name Barbon, when referring to Dr. Barbon, one of the chief rebuilders of the city of London after the Fire. Between Barebones and Barbon is a wide gap, and Barbon's Parliament suggests nothing ludicrous whatsoever. Yet (if we set aside the baptismal name) what an amount of ridicule has been cast over this same Parliament on account of a surname which in reality has been made to meet the occasion. No historian has heaped more sarcasm on the "Rump" than Hume, but he never styles the leatherseller as anything but "Barebone."

But while Praise-God has obtained exceptional notoriety, not so Faint-not, and yet there was a day when Faint-not bade fair to take its place as a regular and recognized name. I should weary the reader did I furnish a full list of instances. Here are a few:

"1585, March 6. Baptized Faynt-not, d. of James Browne."—Warbleton.

"1590, Jan. 17. Baptized Faynt-not Wood."—Cranbrook.

"1631, ——. Thomas Perse married Faint-not Kennarde."—Chiddingly.

"1642, Aug. 2. Married John Pierce and Faint-not Polhill, widow."—Burwash, Sussex.

This Faint-not Polhill was mother of Edward Polhill, a somewhat celebrated writer of his day. She married her first husband December 11, 1616.

"1678, Feb. 12. Buried Faint-not Blatcher, a poor old widdow."—Warbleton.

The rents of certain houses which provided an exhibition for the boys of Lewes Grammar School were paid in 1692 as usual. One item is set down as follows:

"Faint-not Batchelor's house, per annum, £6 0 0."—"Hist. and Ant. Lewes," i. 311.

Faint-not occurs in Maresfield Church ("Suss. Arch. Coll.," xiv. 151). We have already referred to Faint-not, the daughter of "Dudley Fenner, minister of the Word of God" at Marden, Kent.

Fear-not was also in use. The Rector of Warbleton baptized one of his own children by the name; some of his parishioners copied him:

"1594, Nov. 10. Baptized Fear-not, sonne of Richard Maye."

"1589, Oct. 19. Baptized Fear-not, sonne of Willm. Browne."

Decidedly cheerful were such names as Hope-still or Hopeful. Both occur in Banbury Church. Hopeful Wheatley has already been mentioned.

"1611, June 16. Baptized Hope-still, d. to Edward Peedle."

"1697, Dec. 30. Buried Hope-still Faxon, a olde mayde."

Whether or no her matrimonial expectations were still high to the end, we are not told.

One of the earliest Pilgrim Fathers was Hope-still Foster (Hotten, p. 68). He went out to New England about 1620. His name became a common one out there. Two bearers of the name at home lived so long that it reached the Georges:

"Near this place is interred the body of John Warden, of Butler's Green in this parish, Esq., who died April 30, 1730, aged 79 years; and also of Hope-still, his wife, who died July 22, 1749, aged 92."—Cuckfield Church, Sussex.

"Dec. 1, 1714. Administration of goods of Michael Watkins, granted to Hope-still Watkins, his widow."—C. S. P.

In the list of incumbents of Lydney, Gloucestershire, will be found the name of Help-on-high Foxe, who was presented to the living by the Dean and Chapter of Hereford in 1660. For some reason or other, possibly to curtail the length, he styled himself in general as Hope-well, and this was retained on his tomb:

"Hic in Cristo quiescit Hope-wel Foxe, in artibus magister, hujus ecclesiæ vicarius vigilantissimus qui obiit 2 die Aprilis, 1662."—Bigland's "Monuments of Gloucester."

How quickly such names were caught up by parishioners from their clergy may again be seen in the case of Hope-well Voicings, of Tetbury, who left a rentcharge of £1 for the charity schools at Cirencester in 1720. Probably he was christened by the vicar himself at Lydney.

We have already mentioned Rejoice Lord, of Salehurst. The name had a tremendous run:

"1647, June 22. Buried Rejoice, daughter of John Harvey.

"1679, Oct. 18. Baptized Rejoice, daughter of Nicholas Wratten."—Warbleton.

Rejoice reached the eighteenth century:

"1713, Sep. 29. Married John Pimm, of St. Dunstan's, Cant., to Rejoice Epps, of the precincts of this church."—Cant. Cath.

Magnify and Give-thanks frequently occur in Warbleton register:

"1595, Dec. 7. Buried Gyve-thanks Bentham, a child.

"1593, Mch. 11. Baptized Give-thanks, the dather of Thomas Elliard.

"1591, Feb. 6. Baptized Magnyfy, sonne of William Freeland.

"1587, Sep. 17. Baptized Magnyfye, sonne of Thomas Beard.

"1587, April 2. Baptized Give-thankes, sonne of Thomas Cunsted."

It is from the same register we obtain examples of an exhortatory name known to have existed at this time, viz. "Be-thankful." A dozen cases might be cited:

"1586, Feb. 6. Baptized Be-thankfull, the dather of Abell Tyerston.

"1601, Nov. 8. Baptized Be-thankfull, d. of James Gyles.

"1617, Nov. 27. Married Thomas Flatt and Be-thankefull Baker.

"1662, May 9. Buried Be-thankeful Giles."

Thus Miss Giles bore her full name for over sixty years: and, I dare say, was very proud of it. Besides Be-thankful, there was "Be-strong:"

"1592, Nov. 26. Baptized Be-strong Philpott."—Cranbrook.

Many of the exhortatory names related to the fallen nature of man. One great favourite at Warbleton was "Sin-deny." It was coined first by Heley, the Puritan rector, in 1588, for one of his own daughters. Afterwards the entries are numerous. Two occur in one week:

"1592, April 23. Baptized Sin-denye, d. of Richard Tebb.

" " 29. Baptized Sin-denye, d. of William Durant.

"1594, March 9. Baptized Sin-denye, d. of Edward Outtered."

This name seems to have been monopolized by the girls. One instance only to the contrary can

I find:

"1588, Feb. 9. Baptized Sin-dynye, sonne of Andrew Champneye."

Still keeping to the same register, we find of this class:

"1669, Jan. 21. Buried Refrayne Benny, a widdow."

"1586, May 15. Baptized Refrayne, dather of John Celeb."

"1586, April 24. Baptized Repent, sonne of William Durant."

"1587, July 16. Baptized Returne, sonne of Rychard Farret."

"1587, Aug. 6. Baptized Obey, sonne of Rychard Larkford."

"1587, Dec. 24. Baptized Depend, sonne of Edward Outtered."

"1588, Ap. 7. Baptized Feare-God, sonne of John Couper."

"1608, Aug. 14. Baptized Repent Champney, a basterd."

"1595. Maye 18. Baptized Refrayne, d. of John Wykes."

Many registers contain "Repent." Cranbrook has an early one:

"1586, Jan. 1. Baptized Repent Boorman."

Abuse-not is quaint:

"1592, Sep. 17. Baptized Abuse-not, d. of Rychard Ellis."

"1592, Dec. 3. Baptized Abus-not, d. of John Collier."—Warbleton.

The last retained her name:

"1603, Maye 20. Buried Abuse-not Collyer."

Here, again, are two curious entries:

"1636, March 19. Baptized Be-steadfast, sonne of Thomas Elliard."

"1589, Nov. 9. Baptized Learn-wysdome, d. of Rychard Ellis."

These also are extracts from the Warbleton registers. None of them, however, can be more strongly exhortatory than this:

"1660, April 15. Baptized Hate-evill, d. of Antony Greenhill."—Banbury.

Doubtless she was related to William Greenhill, born 1581, the great Puritan commentator on Ezekiel. This cannot be the earliest instance of the name, for one Hate-evill Nutter was a settler in New England twenty years before her baptism (Bowditch). I suspect its origin can be traced to the following:—

"1580, June 25. Baptized Hatill (Hate-ill), sonne of Willm. Wood."

"1608, Nov. 17. Baptized Hatill, sonne to Antony Robinson."—Middleton-Cheney.

As Middleton-Cheney is a mere outlying parish from Banbury, I think we may see whence Hate-evil Greenhill's name was derived.

Returning once more to Warbleton, Lament is so common there, as in other places, that it would be absurd to suppose the mother had died in childbirth in every instance. A glance at the register of deaths disproves the idea. The fact is Lament was used, like Repent, as a serious call to godly sorrow for sin:

"1594, July 22. Baptized Lament, d. of Antony Foxe."

"1598, May 14. Baptized Lament, d. of John Fauterell."

"1600, Mch 29. Baptized Lament, d. of Anne Willard."

But we must not linger too much at Warbleton.

Live-well commanded much attention. Neither sex could claim the monopoly of it, as my examples prove. At the beginning of Charles II.'s reign, a warrant was abroad for the capture of one Live-well Chapman, a seditious printer. In such a charge it is possible he fulfilled the pious injunction of his god-parent:

"1662-3, March 9. Warrant to apprehend Live-well Chapman, with all his printing instruments and materials."—C. S. P.

He is mentioned again:

"1663, Nov. 24. Warrant to Sir Edward Broughton to receive Live-well Chapman, and keep him close prisoner for seditious practices."—C. S. P.

This is no unique case. Live-well Sherwood, an alderman of Norwich, was put on a commission for sequestering papists in 1643 (Scobell's "Orders of Parl.," p. 38).

Again the name occurs:

"1702, Oct. 15. Thomas Halsey, of Shadwell, widower, to Live-well Prisienden, of Stepney."—St. Dionis Backchurch.

Love-God is found twice, at least, for letters of administration in the case of one Love-God Gregory were granted in 1654. Also is found:

"1596, March 6. Baptized Love-God, daughter of Hugh Walker, vicar."—Berwick, Sussex.

Do-good is exhortatory enough, but it rather smacks of works; hence, possibly, the reason why I have only seen it once. A list of the trained bands under Lord Zouch, Lord Warden of Hastings, 1619, includes—

"Musketts, James Knight, Doo-good Fuller, Thomas Pilcher."—"Arch. Soc. Coll." (Sussex), xiv. 102.

Fare-well seems a shade more worldly than Live-well, but was common enough:

"1589, July 16, Baptized Fare-well, son of Thomas Hamlen, gent."—St. Dunstan-in-the-West, London.

"1723, Sep. 5. Buried Mr. Fare-well Perry, rector of St. Peter's."—Marlborough.

A writer in Notes and Queries, September 9, 1865 (Mr. Lloyd of Thurstonville), says—

"A man named Sykes, resident in this locality, had four sons whom he named respectively Love-well, Do-well, Die-well, and Fare-well. Sad to say, Fare-well Sykes met an untimely end by drowning, and was buried this week (eleventh Sunday after Trinity) in Lockwood churchyard. The brothers Live-well, Do-well, and Die-well were the chief mourners on the occasion."

It seems almost impossible that the father should have restored three of the Puritan names accidentally. Probably he had seen or heard of these names in some Yorkshire church register. One of these names, Farewell, is still used in the county, as the directories show. I see Fare-well Wardley, in Sheffield, in the West Riding Directory for 1867.

This closes the exhortatory class. It is both numerous and interesting, and some of its instances grew very familiar, and looked as if they might find a permanent place in our registers. The eighteenth century saw them all succumb, however.

(d.) Accidents of Birth.

Evidently it was a Puritan notion that a quiverful of children was a matter for thanksgiving. There is a pleasant ring in some of the names selected by religious gossips at this time, or witnesses, as I should rather term them. Free-gift was one such, and was on the point of becoming an accepted English name, when the Restoration stepped in, and it had to follow the way of the others. It began with the Presbyterian clergy, judging by the date of its rise:

"1616, ——. Buried Mary, wiffe of Free-gift Mabbe."—Chiddingly, Sussex.

"1621, ——. Baptized John, son of Free-gift Bishopp."—Ditto.

"1591, Jan. 14. Baptized Fre-gift, sonne of Abraham Bayley."—Warbleton.

The will of Free-gift Stacey was proved in 1656 in London; while a subsidy obtained by an unpopular tax on fires, hearths, and stoves in 1670, rates a resident in Chichester thus:

"Free-gift Collins, two hearths."—"Suss. Arch. Coll.," xxiv. 81.

The last instance I have seen is:

"Dec. 4, 1700. The petition of Free-gift Pilkington, wife of Richard Pilkington, late port-master of Ipswich, county Suffolk."—C. S. P.

Good-gift was rarer:

"1618, March 28. Bapt. John, sonne of Goodgift Gynninges."—Warbleton.

One of the earliest Puritan eccentricities was From-above, mentioned by Camden as existing in 1614:

"1582, March 10. Baptized From-above Hendley."—Cranbrook.

A subsidy collected within the rape of Lewes in 1621 records:

"From-above Hendle, gent, in landes, 30 4 0."—"Suss. Arch. Coll.," lx. 71.

Many of these names suggest thanksgiving for an "addition to the family." More-fruit is one such:

"1587, June 6. Baptized More-fruite Stone, of Steven."—Berwick, Sussex.

"1592, Oct. 1. Baptized More-fruite Starre."—Cranbrook.

"1599, Nov. 4. Baptized More-fruite, d. of Richard Barnet."—Warbleton.

"1608, Aug. 28. Baptized More-frute, d. of Rychard Curtes."—Ditto.

We have already referred to More-fruit Fenner, christened about the same time.

The great command to Adam and Eve was, "Multiply, and replenish the earth." Some successor of Thomas Heley thought it no harm to emphasize this at the font:

"1677, May 14. Buried Replenish, ye wife of Robert French."

But "Increase" or "Increased" was the representative of this class of thanksgiving names, in palpable allusion to Psa. cxv. 14:

"The Lord shall increase you more and more, you and your children."

I could easily furnish the reader with half a hundred instances. It is probable Thomas Heley was the inventor of it. The earliest example I can find is that of his own child:

"1587, March 26. Baptized Increased, dather of Thomas Helley, minister."

"1637, Sep. 15. Buried Increase, wife of Robard Barden."

"1589, Apr. 13. Baptized Increased, d. of John Gynninges."—Warbleton.

One or two instances from other quarters may be noted:

"1660, June. Petition of Increased Collins, for restoration to the keepership of Mote's Bulwark, Dover."—C. S. P.

Dr. Increase Mather, of the Liverpool family of that name, will be a familiar figure to every student of Puritan history. In 1685 he returned from America to thank King James for the Toleration Act. Through him it became a popular name in New England, although Increase Nowell, who obtained a charter of appropriation of Massachusetts Bay, March 4, 1628, and emigrated from London, may have helped in the matter (Neal's "New England," p. 124).

The perils of childbirth are marked in the thanksgiving name of Deliverance. So early as 1627 the will of Deliverance Wilton was proved in London. Camden, too, writing in 1614, says "Delivery" was known to him; while Adams, whose Puritan proclivities I have previously hinted at, preaching in London in 1626, asserts that Safe-deliverance existed to his knowledge ("Meditations upon the Creed"). Deliverance crossed the Atlantic with the Pilgrim Fathers (Bowditch), and I see one instance, at least, in Hotten's "Emigrants:"

"1670, Feb. 18. Buried Deliverance Addison."—Christ Church, Barbados.

"Deliverance Hobbs and Deliverance Dane were both examined in the great trial for witchcraft at Salem, June 2, 1692."—Neal, "New England," pp. 533, 506.

The last instance, probably, at home is—

"1757, Jan. 7. Buried Deliverance Branan."—Donnybrook, Dublin (Notes and Queries).

This "Deliverance" must have been especially common. One more instance: in the will of Anne Allport, sen., of Cannock, Stafford, dated March 25, 1637, mention is made of "my son-in-law Deliverance Fennyhouse" (vide Notes and Queries, Dec. 8, 1860, W. A. Leighton).

Much-mercy is characteristic:

"1598, May 22. Baptized Much-mercie Harmer, a child."—Warbleton.

This is but one more proof of Heley's influence, for he had baptized one of his own sons "Much-mercy"" in 1585.

Perhaps a sense of undeserved mercies caused the following:

"1589, Sep. 28. Baptized No-merit, dather of Stephen Vynall."—Warbleton.

That babes are cherubs, if not seraphs, every mother knows; but it is not often the fact is recorded in our church registers. Peculiar thankfulness must have been felt here:

"On Dec. 11, 1865, aged seventy-eight years, died Cherubin Diball."—Notes and Queries, 4th Series, ii. 130.

And two hundred years previously, i.e. 1678, Seraphim Marketman is referred to in the last testament of John Kirk. But was it gratitude, after all? We have all heard of the wretched father who would persist in having the twins his wife presented to him christened by the names of Cherubin and Seraphim, on the ground that "they continually do cry." Perhaps Cherubin Diball and Seraphim Marketman made noise enough for two!

But if the father of the twins was not as thankful for his privilege as he ought to have been, others were. Thanks and Thankful were not unknown to our forefathers. One of the earliest instances I can find is the marriage lines of Thankful Hepden:

"1646, July 16. Thankfull Hepden and Fraunces Bruer."—St. Dionis Backchurch.

In Peck's "Desiderata Curiosa" (p. 537) we read:

"Dec. M.D.CLVI. Mr. Thankful Frewen's corps carried through London, to be interred in Sussex."

Thankful's father was John Frewen, Rector of Northiam, the eminent Puritan already referred to. Accepted, the elder son's name, belongs to this same class. Thankful seems to have become a favourite in that part of the country, and to have lingered for a considerable time. In the "History of the Town and Port of Rye" we find (p. 466):

"Christmas, 1723. Assessment for repairs of highways: Mr. Thankful Bishop paid 7s 6d."

Again, so late as 1749 we find the death of another Thankful Frewen recorded, who had been Rector of Northiam for sixteen years, christened, no doubt, in memory of his predecessor of a century gone by. Thankful Owen was brother to Gracious Owen, president of St. John's, Oxford, 1650-1660.

One more instance will suffice. The will of Thanks Tilden was proved in 1698. No wonder the name was sufficiently familiar to be embodied in one of the political skits of the Commonwealth period:

"'O, very well said,' quoth Con;
'And so will I do,' says Frank;
And Mercy cries 'Aye,' and Mat, 'Really,'
'And I'm o' that mind,' quoth Thank."

Possibly the sentence "unfeignedly thankful" suggested the other word also; any way, it existed:

"1586, April 1. Baptized Unfeigned, sonne of Roger Elliard."—Warbleton.

The estate of Unfeigned Panckhurst was administered upon in 1656.

From every side we see traces of the popularity of Thankful. During the restoration of Hawkhurst Church, a small tombstone was discovered below the floor, with an inscription to the "memory of Elizabeth, daughter of Thankful Bishop, of Hawkhurst, gent., who died January 2, 1680" ("Arch. Cant.," iv. 108). In the churchwarden's book of the same place occurs this curious item:

"1675. Received by Thankfull Thorpe, churchwarden in the year 1675, of Richard Sharpe of Bennenden, the summe of one pound for shouting of a hare."—"Arch. Cant.," v. 75.

Several names seem to breathe assurance and trust in imminent peril. Perhaps both mother and child were in danger. Preserved is distinctly of this class:

"Here lieth the body of Preserved, the daughter of Thomas Preserved Emms, who departed this life in the 18th year of her age, on the 17th of November, MDCCXII."—St. Nicholas, Yarmouth.

"1588, Aug. 1. Baptized Preserved, sonne of Thomas Holman.

"1594, Nov. 17. Baptized Preserved, sonne of Roger Caffe."—Warbleton.

Preserved Fish, whose name appeared for many years in the New York Directory, did not get his name this way. A friend of his informs me that, about eighty-five years ago, a vessel was wrecked on the New Jersey coast, and when washed ashore, a little child was discovered secured in one of the berths, the only living thing left. The finder named the boy "Preserved Fish," and he bore it through a long and honoured life to the grave, having made for himself a good position in society.

Beloved would naturally suggest itself to grateful parents:

"1672, July 10. Buried Anne, wife of Beeloved King."—Warbleton.

This name is also found in St. Matthew, Friday Street, London.

Joy-in-Sorrow is the story of Rachel and Benoni over again:

"1595. On the last daye of August the daughter of Edward Godman was baptized and named Joye-in-Sorrow."—Isfield, Sussex.

Lamentation tells its own tale, unless taken from the title of one of the Old Testament books:

"Plaintiff, Lamentation Chapman: Bill to stay proceedings on a bond relating to a tenement and lands in the parish of Borden, Kent."—"Proc. in Chancery, Eliz.," i. 149.

We have already mentioned Safe-on-high Hopkinson, christened at Salehurst in 1591, and Help-on-high Foxe, incumbent of Lydney, Gloucester, in 1661. The former died a few days after baptism, and the event seems to have been anticipated in the name selected.

The termination on-high was popular. Stand-fast-on-high Stringer dwelt at Crowhurst, in Sussex, about the year 1635, as will be proved shortly, and Aid-on-high is twice met with:

"1646, June 6. Letters of administration taken out in the estate of Margery Maddock, of Ross, Hereford, by Aid-on-high Maddock, her husband."

"1596, July 19. Stephen Vynall had a sonne baptized, and was named Aid-on-hye."—Isfield, Sussex.

The three following are precatory, and we may infer that the life of either mother or child was endangered:

"1618, ——. Married Restore Weekes to Constant Semar."—Chiddingly.

"1613, ——. Baptized Have-mercie, d. of Thomas Stone."—Berwick, Sussex.

A monument at Cobham, Surrey, commemorates the third:

"Hereunder lies interred the body of Aminadab Cooper, citizen and merchaunt taylor of London, who left behind him God-helpe, their only sonne. Hee departed this life the 23d June, 1618."

Still less hopeful of augury was the following:

"1697, July 6. Weakly Ekins, citizen and grocer, London."—"Inquisit. of Lunacy," Rec. Office MSS.

What about him? His friends brought him forward as a case for the Commissioners of Lunacy to take in hand, on the ground that he was weak of intellect, and unfit to manage his business. It might be asked whether such a name was not likely to drive him to the state specified in the petition.

While on the subject of birth, we may notice that the Presbyterian clergy were determined to visit the sins of the parents on the children in cases of illegitimacy. A few instances must suffice:

"1589, Aug. 3. Baptized Helpless Henley, a bastard."—Berwick, Sussex.

"1608, Aug. 14. Baptized Repent Champney, a bastard."—Warbleton.

"1599, May 13. Baptized Repentance, d. of Martha Henley, a bastard."—Warbleton.

"1600, Mch. 26. Baptized Lament, d. of Anne Willard, a bastard."—Ditto.

"1600, April 13. Baptized Repentance Gilbert, a bastard."—Cranbrook.

"1598, Jan. 27. Baptized Forsaken, filius meretricis Agnetis Walton."—Sedgefield.

"1609, Dec. 17. Baptized Flie-fornication, the bace son of Catren Andrewes."—Waldron.

This is more kindly, but an exceptional case:

"1609, Nov. 25. Baptized Fortune, daughter of Dennis Judie, and in sin begoten."—Middleton-Cheney.

(e.) General.

There is a batch of names which was especially common, and which hardly appears to be of Puritan origin; I mean names presaging good fortune. Doubtless, however, they were at first used, in a purely spiritual sense, of the soul's prosperity; and afterwards, by more worldly minds, were referred to the good things of this life.

Fortune became a great favourite:

"1607, Oct. 4. Baptized Fortune Gardyner."—St. Giles, Camberwell.

"1642, ——. Baptized Fortune, daughter of Thomas Patchett."—Ludlow, Shropshire.

"1652-3, Mch. 10. Married Mr. John Barrington and Mrs. Fortune Smith."—St. Dionis Backchurch.

"1723, April 8. Buried Fortune Symons, aged 111 years."—Hammersmith.

If Fortune meant fulness of years, it was attained in this last example.

Wealthy is equally curious:

"1665 [no date]. Petition of Wealthy, lawful wife of Henry Halley, and one of the Duke of York's guards."—C. S. P.

"1714, April 25. Buried Wealthy Whathing."—Donnybrook, Dublin.

"1704, Aug. 18, died Riches Browne, gent., aged 62."—Scarning, Norfolk.

The father of this Riches was also Riches, and was married to the daughter of John Nabs! (vide Blomefield, vi. 5).

Several names may be set in higgledy-piggledy fashion, for they belong to no class, and are sui generis.

Pleasant is found several times:

"1681, Nov. 8. Christened Pleasant, daughter of Robert Tarlton."—St. Dionis Backchurch.

"1725, Dec. 18. William Whiteing, of Chislett, to Pleasant Burt, of Reculver."—Cant. Cath.

"1728, Nov. 3. Buried Pleasant Smith, late wife of Mr. John Smith."—St. Dionis Backchurch.

The following, no doubt, had a political as well as spiritual allusion. It occurs several times in the New York Directory of the present year:

"1689, March 4. Petition of Freeman Howes, controller of Chichester port."—"C. S. P. Treasury."

"1691, Sep. 21. Petition of Freeman Collins."—Ditto.

"1661. Petition of Freeman Sonds."—"C. S. P. Domestic."

What a freak of fancy is commemorated in the following:

"1698, June 23. Examination of Isaac Cooper, Thomas Abraham, and Centurian Lucas."—C.

S. P.

"1660, June. Petition of Handmaid, wife of Aaron Johnson."—C. S. P.

"1661, August 29. Baptized Miracle, son of George Lessa."—New Buckenham.

"1728. Married John Foster to Beulah Digby."—Somerset House Chapel.

The Trinity in Unity were not held in proper reverence; for Trinity Langley fought in the army of Cromwell, while Unity Thornton (St. James, Piccadilly, 1680) and Unity Awdley ("Top. et. Gen.," viii. 201) appear a little later:

"1694, Jan. 8. James Commelin to Mrs. Unitie Awdrey."—Market Lavington.

"1668, Feb. 15. Baptized Unity, son of John Brooks."—Banbury.

Providence Hillershand died August 14, 1749, aged 72 (Bicknor, Gloucester). Providence was a he.

"1752, Nov. 5. Buried Selah, d. of Ric. and Diana Collins."—Dyrham, Gloucestershire.

"1586, April 10. Baptized My-sake Hallam."—Cranbrook.

Biblical localities were much resorted to:

"1616, Nov. 26. Baptized Bethsaida, d. of Humphrey Trenouth."—St. Columb Major.

"1700, June 6. Buried Canaan, wife of John Hatton, 55 years."—Forthampton, Gloucestershire.

"1706, April 27. Married Eden Hardy to Esther Pantall."—St. Dionis Backchurch.

"1695, Dec. 15. Baptized Richard, son of Richard and Nazareth Rudde."—St. James, Piccadilly.

Nazareth Godden's will was administrated upon in 1662. Battalion Shotbolt was defendant in a suit in the eleventh year of Queen Anne (Decree Rolls, Record Office). The following is odd:

"1683, Oct. 11. Buried Mr. Inward Ansloe."—Cant. Cath.

V. A Scoffing World.

While these strange pranks were being played, the world was not asleep. Calamy seems to have discovered a source of melancholy satisfaction in the fact that the quaint names of his brethren were subjected to the raillery of a wicked world. One of the ejected ministers was Sabbath Clark, minister of Tarvin, Cheshire. Of him he writes:

"He had been constant minister of the parish for nigh upon sixty years. He carried Puritanism in his very name, by which his good father intended he should bear the memorial of God's Holy Day. This was a course that some in those times affected, baptizing their children Reformation, Discipline, etc., as the affections of their parents stood engaged. For this they have sufficiently suffered from Profane Wits, and this worthy person did so in particular. Yet his name was not a greater offence to such persons than his holy life."

Probably Calamy was referring to the "profane wit" Dr. Cosin, Bishop of Chester, who, in a visitation held at Warrington about the year 1643, is said to have acted as follows:—

"A minister, called Sabbaith Clerke, the Doctor re-baptized, took's marke, and call'd him Saturday."

That this was a deliberate insult, and not a pleasantry, Calamy, of course, would stoutly maintain. Hence the above sample of holy ire.

Many of the names in the list I have recorded must have met with the good-humoured raillery of the every-day folk the strangely stigmatized bearer might meet. I suppose in good time, however, the owner, and the people he was accustomed to mix with, got used to it. It is true they must have resorted, not unfrequently, to curter forms, much after the fashion of the now almost forgotten nick forms of the Plantagenet days. Fight-the-good-fight-of-faith is a very large mouthful, if you come to try it, and I dare say Mr. White or Brown, whoever he might be, did not so strongly urge as he ought to have done the gross impropriety of his friends recognizing him by the simple style of "Faith" or "Fight." Fancy at a dinner, in a day that had not invented the convenient practice of calling a man by his surname, having to address a friend across the table, "Please, Fight-the-good-fight-of-faith, pass the pepper!" The thing was impossible. Even Help-on-high was found cumbersome, and, as we have seen, the Rector of Lydney curtailed it.

A curious instance of waggery anent this matter of length will be found in the register of St. Helen, Bishopgate. The entry is dated 1611, just the time when the dramatists were making fun of this Puritanic innovation, and when the custom was most popular:

"Sept. 1, 1611. Job-rakt-out-of-the-asshes, being borne the last of August in the lane going to Sir John Spencer's back-gate, and there laide in a heape of seacole asshes, was baptized the ffirst day of September following, and dyed the next day after."

This is confirmed by the burial records:

"Sept. 2, 1611. Job-rakt-out-of-the-asshes, as is mentioned in the register of christenings."

The reference, of course, is to Job ii. 8:

"And he took him a potsherd to scrape himself withal; and he sat down among the ashes."

This was somewhat grim fun, though. Probably Job-rakt-out-of-the-asshes, during his brief life, would be styled by the curter title of "Ashes." It is somewhat curious to notice that Camden, writing three years later, says Ashes existed. Perhaps this was the instance.

A similar instance of waggery is found in the parish church of Old Swinford, where the following entry occurs:—

"1676, Jan. 18. Baptized Dancell-Dallphebo-Marke-Antony-Dallery-Gallery-Cesar, sonn of Dancell-Dallphebo-Marke-Antony-Dallery-Gallery-Cesar Williams."

Allowing the father to be thirty years of age, the paternal christening would take place in 1646, which would be a likely time in the political history of England for a mimical hit at Puritan eccentricity.

(a.) The Playwrights.

There is a capital scene in "The Ordinary" (1634), where Andrew Credulous, after trolling out a verse of nonsensical rhyme against the Puritan names, says to his friends Hearsay and Slicer, in allusion to these new long and uncouth names:

"Andrew the Great Turk?
I would I were a peppercorn, if that
It sounds not well. Doe'st not?
Slicer. Yes, very well.
Credulous. I'll make it else great Andrew Mahomet,
Imperious Andrew Mahomet Credulous.

Tell me which name sounds best.

Hearsay. That's as you speak 'em.

Credulous. Oatmealman Andrew! Andrew Oatmealman!

Hearsay. Ottoman, sir, you mean.

Credulous. Yes, Ottoman."

"Oatmealman Andrew! Andrew Oatmealman!" seems to have suggested to Thomson that unfortunate line:

"O Sophonisba, Sophonisba O,"

so unkindly parodied into—

"O Jemmy Thomson, Jemmy Thomson O."

From this quotation it will be seen that it is not to the church register alone we must turn, to discover the manner in which these new names were being received by the public. Calamy might wax wroth over the "profane wits" of the day, but one of the severest blows administered to the men he has undertaken to defend, came from his own side; for Thomas Adams, Rector of St. Benet, Paul's Wharf, must unquestionably be placed, even by Calamy's own testimony, among the Puritan clergy of his day. His name does not appear in the list of silenced clergy, and his works are dedicated to pronounced friends of the Noncomformist cause. In his "Meditations upon the Creed" (vol. iii. p. 213, edit. 1872), first published in 1629, he says—

"Some call their sons Emanuel: this is too bold. The name is proper to Christ, therefore not to be communicated to any creature. It is no less than presumption to give a subject's son the style of his prince. Yea, it seems to me not fit for Christian humility to call a man Gabriel or Michael, giving the names of angels to the sons of mortality.

"On the other side, it is a petulant absurdity to give them ridiculous names, the very rehearsing whereof causeth laughter. There be certain affectate names which mistaken zeal chooseth for honour, but the event discovers a proud singularity. It was the speech of a famous prophet, Non sum melior patribus meis—'I am no better than my fathers;' but such a man will be sapientior patribus suis—'Wiser than his fathers.' As if they would tie the goodness of the person to the signification of the name. But still a man is what he is, not what he is called; he were the same, with or without that title or that name. And we have known Williams and Richards, names not found in sacred story, but familiar to our country, prove as gracious saints as any Safe-deliverance, Fight-the-good-fight-of-faith, or such like, which have been rather descriptions than names."

I have quoted portions of this before. I have now given it in full, for it is trenchant, and full of common sense. Coming from the quarter it did, we cannot doubt it had its effect in throwing the practice into disfavour among the better orders. But there had been a continued battery going on from a foe by whose side Adams would have rather faced death than fight. Years before he wrote his own sentiments, the Puritan nomenclature had been roughly handled on the stage, and by such ruthless pens as Ben Jonson, Cowley, and Beaumont and Fletcher. A year before little Job-rakt-out-of-the-asshes was laid to rest, the sharp and unsparing sarcasm of "The Alchemist" and "Bartholomew Fair" had been levelled at these doings. The first of these two dramas Ben Jonson saw acted in 1610. By that time the custom was a generation old, and men who bore the godly but uncouth sobriquets were walking the streets, keeping shops, driving bargains, known, if not avoided, of all men. In 1610 Increase Brown, your apprentice, might be demanding an advance upon his wages, Help-on-high Jones might be imploring your patronage, while Search-the-Scriptures Robinson might be diligently studying his ledger to see how he could swell his total against you for tobacco and groceries. In 1610 society would be really awake to the fact that such things existed, and proceed to discuss this serio-comic matter in a comico-serious manner. The time was exactly ripe for the playwright, and it was the fate of the Presbyterians that the playwright was "rare Ben."

In "The Alchemist" appears Ananias, a deacon, who is thus questioned by Subtle:
"What are you, sir?
Ananias. Please you, a servant of the exiled brethren,
That deal with widows' and with orphans' goods,
And make a just account unto the saints:
A deacon.
Subtle. O, you are sent from Master Wholesome,
Your teacher?
Ananias. From Tribulation Wholesome,
Our very zealous pastor."

After accusing Ananias of being related to the "varlet that cozened the Apostles," Subtle meets Tribulation himself, the Amsterdam pastor, whom he treats with scant courtesy:
"Nor shall you need to libel 'gainst the prelates,
And shorten so your ears against the hearing
Of the next wire-drawn grace. Nor of necessity
Rail against plays, to please the alderman
Whose daily custard you devour; nor lie
With zealous rage till you are hoarse. Not one
Of these so singular arts. Nor call yourselves
By name of Tribulation, Persecution,
Restraint, Long-patience, and such like, affected
By the whole family or wood of you,
Only for glory, and to catch the ear
Of your disciple."

To which hard thrust Tribulation meekly makes response:
"Truly, sir, they are
Ways that the godly brethren have invented
For propagation of the glorious cause."

Every word of this harangue of Subtle's would tell upon a sympathetic audience. So popular was the play itself, that a common street song was made out of it, the first verse of which we find Credulous singing in "The Ordinary:"

"My name's not Tribulation,
Nor holy Ananias;
I was baptized in fashion,
Our vicar did hold bias."
Act iv. sc. 1.

This comedy appeared twenty years after "The Alchemist," and yet the song was still popular. Many a lad with a Puritan name must have had these rhymes flung into his teeth. Tribulation, by the way, is one of the names given in Camden's list, written four years later than Ben Jonson's play. This name, which has been the object of an antiquary's, a playwright's, a ballad-monger's and an historian's ridicule (for Macaulay had his fling at it), curiously enough I have not found in the registers. But its equivalent, Lamentation, occurs, as we have seen, in the "Chancery Suits" (1590-1600), in the case of Lamentation Chapman. Restraint is met by Abstinence Pougher, and Persecution by Trial Travis (C. S. P. 1619, June 7).

Still more severe, again, is this same dramatist in "Bartholomew Fair," which was performed in London, October, 1614, by the retinue of Lady Elizabeth, James's daughter. Pouring ridicule upon the butt of the day, whose name of "Puritan" was by-and-by to be anagrammatized into "a turnip," from the cropped roundness of his head, this drama became the play-goers' favourite. It was suppressed during the Commonwealth, and one of the first to be revived at the Restoration. The king is said to have given special orders for its performance. Whether his grandfather liked it as much may be doubted, for it once or twice touches on doctrinal points, and James thought he had a special gift for theology.

Zeal-of-the-land Busy is a Banbury man, which town was then even more celebrated for Puritans than cakes. Caster, in "The Ordinary," says—

"I'll send some forty thousand unto Paul's:
Build a cathedral next in Banbury:
Give organs to each parish in the kingdom."

Zeal-of-the-land is thus inquired of by Winwife:

"What call you the reverend elder you told me of, your Banbury man?

Littlewit. Rabbi Busy, sir: he is more than an elder, he is a prophet, sir.

Quarlous. O, I know him! a baker, is he not?

Littlewit. He was a baker, sir, but he does dream now, and see visions: he has given over his trade.

Quarlous. I remember that, too: out of a scruple that he took, in spiced conscience, those cakes he made were served to bridales, maypoles, morrices, and such profane feasts and meetings. His christian name is Zeal-of-the-land?

Littlewit. Yes, sir; Zeal-of-the-land Busy.

Winwife. How! what a name's there!

Littlewit. O, they all have such names, sir: he was witness for Win here—they will not be called godfathers—and named her Win-the-fight: you thought her name had been Winnifred, did you not?

Winwife. I did indeed.

Littlewit. He would have thought himself a stark reprobate if it had."

All this would be caviare to the Cavalier, and it is doubtful whether he did not enjoy it more than his grandparents, who could but laugh at it as a hit religious, rather than political. The allusion to witnesses reminds us of Corporal Oath, who in "The Puritan," published in 1607 (Act ii. sc. 3), rails at the zealots for the mild character of their ejaculations. The expression "Oh!" was the most terrible expletive they permitted themselves to indulge in, and some even shook their heads at a brother who had thus far committed himself:

"Why! has the devil possessed you, that you swear no better,

You half-christened c——s, you un-godmothered varlets?"

The terms godfather and godmother were rejected by the disaffected clergy, and they would have the answer made in the name of the sponsors, not the child. Hence they styled them witnesses.

In "Women Pleased," a tragi-comedy, written, as is generally concluded, by Fletcher alone about the year 1616, we find the customary foe of maypoles addressing the hobby:

"I renounce it,

And put the beast off thus, the beast polluted.

And now no more shall Hope-on-high Bomby

Follow the painted pipes of worldly pleasures,

And with the wicked dance the Devil's measures:

Away, thou pampered jade of vanity!"

Here, again, is no exaggeration of name, for we have Help-on-high Foxe to face Hope-on-high Bomby. The Rector of Lydney would be about twenty-five when this play was written, and may have suggested himself the sobriquet. The names are all but identical.

From "Women Pleased" and Fletcher to "Cutter of Coleman Street" and Cowley is a wide jump, but we must make it to complete our quotations from the playwrights. Although brought out after the Restoration, the fun about names was not yet played out. The scene is laid in London in 1658. This comedy was sorely resented by the zealots, and led the author to defend himself in his preface. He says that he has been accused of "prophaneness:"

"There is some imitation of Scripture phrases: God forbid! There is no representation of the true face of Scripture, but only of that vizard which these hypocrites draw upon it."

This must have been more trying to bear even than Cutter himself. Under a thin disguise, Colonel Fear-the-Lord Barebottle is none other than Praise-God Barebone, of then most recent notoriety. Cowley's allusion to him through the medium of Jolly is not pleasant:

"Jolly. My good neighbour, I thank him, Colonel Fear-the-Lord Barebottle, a Saint and a Soap-boiler, brought it. But he's dead, and boiling now himself, that's the best of 't; there's a Cavalier's comfort."

Cutter turns zealot, and wears a most puritanical habit. To the colonel's widow, Mistress Tabitha Barebottle, he says—

"Sister Barebottle, I must not be called Cutter any more: that is a name of Cavalier's darkness;

the Devil was a Cutter from the beginning: my name is now Abednego. I had a vision which whispered to me through a keyhole, 'Go, call thyself Abednego.'"

But Cutter—we beg his pardon, Abednego—was but a sorry convert. Having lapsed into a worldly mind again, he thus addresses Tabitha:

"Shall I, who am to ride the purple dromedary, go dressed like Revelation Fats, the basket-maker?—Give me the peruke, boy!"

I fancy the reader will agree with me that Cowley needed all the arguments he could urge in his preface to meet the charge of irreverence.

(b.) The Sussex Jury.

One of the strongest indictments to be found against this phase of Puritanic eccentricity is to be found in Hume's well-known quotation from Brome's "Travels into England"—a quotation which has caused much angry contention. The book quoted by the historian is entitled "Travels over England, Scotland, and Wales, by James Brome, M.A., Rector of Cheriton, in Kent." Writing soon after the Restoration, Mr. Brome says (p. 279)—

"Before I leave this county (Sussex), I shall subjoin a copy of a Jury returned here in the late rebellious troublesome times, given me by the same worthy hand which the Huntingdon Jury was: and by the christian names then in fashion we may still discover the superstitious vanity of the Puritanical Precisians of that age."

A second list in the British Museum Mr. Lower considers to be of a somewhat earlier date. We will set them side by side:

I dare say ninety-five per cent. of readers of Hume's "History of England" have thought this list of Sussex jurors a silly and extravagant hoax. They are "either a forgery or a joke," says an indignant writer in Notes and Queries. Hume himself speaks of them as names adopted by converts, evidently unaware that these sobriquets were all but invariably affixed at the font. The truth of the matter is this. The names are real enough; the panel is not necessarily so. They are a collection of names existing in several Sussex villages at one and the same time. Everything vouches for their authenticity. The list was printed by Brome while the majority must be supposed still to be living; the villages in which they resided are given, the very villages whose registers we now turn to for Puritanic examples, with the certainty of unearthing them; above all, some of the names can be "run down" even now. Accepted or Approved Frewen, of Northiam, we have already referred to. Free-gift Mabbs, of Chiddingly, is met by the following entry from Chiddingly Church:

"1616, ——. Buried Mary, wife of Free-gift Mabbs."

The will of Redeemed Compton, of Battle, was proved in London in 1641. Restore Weeks, of Cuckfield, is, no doubt, the individual who got married not far away, in Chiddingly Church:

"1618, ——. Restore Weeks espoused Constant Semer."

"Increase Weeks, of Cuckfield," may therefore be accepted as proven, especially as I have shown Increase to be a favourite Puritan name. These two would be brothers, or perchance father and son. As for the other names, the majority have already figured in this chapter. Fly-fornication is still found in Waldron register, though the surname is a different one. Return, Faint-not, Much-mercy, Be-thankful, Repentance, Safe-on-high, Renewed, and More-fruit, all have had their duplicates in the pages preceding. "Fight-the-good-fight-of-faith White, of Emer," is the only unlikely sobriquet left to be dealt with. Thomas Adams, in his "Meditations upon the Creed," in a passage already quoted, testified to its existence in 1629. The conclusion is irresistible: the names are authentic, and the panel may have been.

(c.) Royalists with Puritan Names.

It may be asked whether or not the world went beyond scoffing. Was the stigma of a Puritan name a hindrance to the worldly advancement of the bearer? It is pleasant, in contradiction of any such theory, to quote the following:—

"1663, Aug. Petition of Arise Evans to the King for an order that he may receive £20 in completion of the £70 given him by the King."—C. S. P.

In a second appeal made March, 1664 (C. S. P.), Arise reminds Charles of many "noble acts" done for him as a personal attendant during his exile.

"1660, June. Petition of Handmaid, wife of Aaron Johnson, cabinet-maker, for the place for her husband of Warden in the Tower, he being eminently loyal.

"1660, June. Petition of Increased Collins, His Majesty's servant, for restoration to the keepership of Mote's Bulwark, near Dover, appointed January, 1629, and dismissed in 1642, as not trustworthy, imprisoned and sequestered, and in 1645 tried for his life.

"1660, Oct. Petition of Noah Bridges, and his son Japhet Bridges, for office of clerk to the House of Commons."—C. S. P.

Thus it will be seen that, in the general rush for places of preferment at the Restoration, there were men and women bearing names of the most marked Puritanism, who did not hesitate to forward their appeals with the Williams and Richards of the world at large. They manifestly did not suppose their sobriquets would be any bar to preferment. One of them, too, had been body-man to Charles in his exile, and another had suffered in person and estate as a devoted adherent of royalty. We may hope and trust, therefore, that all this scoffing was of a good-humoured character.

It was, doubtless, the prejudice against Puritan eccentricity that introduced civil titles as font names into England—a class specially condemned by Cartwright and his friends. At any rate, they are contemporary with the excesses of fanatic nomenclature, and are found just in the districts where the latter predominated. Squire must have arisen before Elizabeth died:

"1626, March 21. Petition of Squire Bence."—C. S. P.

"1662, Oct. 30. Baptized Jane, d. of Squire Brockhall."—Hornby, York.

"1722, July 28. Baptized Squire, son of John Pysing and Bennet, his wife."—Cant. Cath.

Duke was the christian name of Captain Wyvill, a fervent loyalist, and grandson of Sir Marmaduke Wyvill, Bart., of Constable Burton, Yorkshire:

"1681, Feb. 12. Baptized Duke, son of Robert Fance, Knt."—Cant. Cath.

Squire passed over the Atlantic, and is frequently to be seen in the States; so that if men may not squire themselves at the end of their names in the great republic, they may at the beginning.

Yorkshire and Lancashire are the great centres for this class of names on English soil. Squire is found on every page of the West Riding Directory, such entries as Squire Jagger, Squire Whitley, Squire Hind, Squire Hardy, or Squire Chapman being of the commonest occurrence. Duke is also a favourite, Duke Redmayne and Duke Oldroyd meeting my eye after turning but half a dozen pages. But the great rival of Squire is Major. There is a kind of martial, if not braggadocio, air about the very sound, which has taken the ear of the Yorkshire folk. Close together I light upon Major Pullen, farmer; Major Wold, farmer; Major Smith, sexton; Major Marshall, ironmonger. Other illustrations are Prince Jewitt, Earl Moore, Marshall Stewart, and Admiral Fletcher. This custom has led to awkwardnesses. There was living at Burley, near Leeds, a short time ago, a "Sir Robert Peel." In the same way "Earl Grey" is found. Sir Isaac Newton was living not long ago in the parish of Soho, London. Robinson Cruso still survives, hale and hearty, at King's Lynn, and Dean Swift is far from dead, as the West Riding Directory proves.

It was an odd idea that suggested "Shorter." I have five instances of it, two from the Westminster Abbey registers:

"1689, March 3. Buried Shorter Norris."

"1690, July 9. Baptized Shorter, son of Robert and Ann Tanner."

Junior is found so early as 1657:

"1657, ———. Christened Junior, sonne of Robert Naze."—Cant. Cath.

Little is similarly used. Little Midgley in the West Riding Directory is scarcely a happy conjunction. In the same town are to be seen John Berry, side by side with "Young John Berry," and Allen Mawson, with Young Allen Mawson.

VI. Bunyan's Debt to the Puritans.

But if the Sussex jury was not visionary, except for the panel, neither was that at Mansoul! What a text is this for the next biographer of Bunyan, if he have the courage to enter upon it! To suggest that the great dreamer was not a reprobate in his youth, and thus spoil the contrast between his converted and unconverted life, was a perilous act on Lord Macaulay's part. To insinuate that he had a not altogether unpleasant time of it in the Bedford gaol, that he could have his friends to visit him, and, on the face of it, ink, paper, and quills to set down his meditations, even this is enough to set a section of political and religious society about our ears. But to hint that his character names were not wholly the offspring of his imagination, not thought out in the isolation of his dreary captivity, and not pictured in his brain, while his brain-pan was lying upon a hard and comfortless pallet—this, I know, not very long ago would have brought a mob about me! In the present day, I shall only be smiled upon with contempt, and condemned to a righteous ignominy by the superior judgment of the worshippers of John Bunyan!

Nevertheless I ask, were the great mass of Bunyan's character names the creation of his own brain, or were they suggested by the nomenclature of his friends or neighbours in the days of his youth? It is the peculiarity of the names in the "Pilgrim's Progress" and "Siege of Mansoul," that they suggest the incidents of which the bearers are the heroes. But, in a large proportion of cases, these names already existed. Born in 1628, Bunyan saw Puritan character names at their climax. Living at Elstow, he was within the limits of the district most addicted to the practice. He had seen Christian and Hopeful, Christiana and Mercy, of necessity long before he was "haled to prison" at Bedford. The four fair damsels, Discretion, Piety, Charity, and Prudence, may and must have in part been his companions in his boyish rambles years before he met them in the Valley of Humiliation; and if afterwards, in the Siege of Mansoul, he turned Charity into a man, he was only doing what godfathers and godmothers had been doing for thirty years previously. The name and sweet character of Faithful might be a personal reminiscence, good Father Honest a quondam host on one of his preaching expeditions, and Standfast, "that right good pilgrim," an old Pædo-Baptist of his acquaintance. The shepherds Watchful, Sincere, and Experience, if not Knowledge, were known of all men, in less pastoral avocations. And as for the men that were panelled in the trial of the Diabolonians, we might set them side by side with the Sussex jury, and certainly the contrast for oddity would be in favour of the cricketing county. Messrs. Belief, True-heart, Upright, Hate-bad, Love-God, See-truth, Heavenly-mind, Thankful, Good-work, Zeal-for-God, and Humble have all, or well-nigh all, been quoted in this chapter, as registered by the church clerk a generation before Do-right, the town-clerk of Mansoul, called them over in court. "Do-right" himself is met by "Do-good," and the witness "Search-truth" by "Search-the-Scriptures." Even "Giant Despair" may have suffered convulsions in teething in the world of fact, before his fits took him in the world of dreams; and his wife "Diffidence" will be found, I doubt not, to have been at large before Bunyan "laid him down in a den." Where names of evil repute come—and they are many—we do not expect to see their duplicates in the flesh. Graceless, Love-lust, Live-loose, Hold-the-world, and Talkative were not names for the Puritan, but their contraries were. Grace meets the case of Grace-less, Love-lust may be set by "Fly-fornication," and Live-loose by "Live-well" or "Continent." Hold-the-world is directly suggested by the favourite "Safe-on-high;" Talkative, by "Silence."

That John Bunyan is under debt to the Puritans for many of his characters must be unquestionable; and were he living now, or could we interview him where he is, I do not doubt we could extract from him, good honest man, the ready admission that in the names of the personages that flit before us in his unapproachable allegory, and which have charmed the fancy of old and young for so many generations, he was merely stereotyping the recollections of childhood, and commemorating, so far as sobriquets were concerned, the companionships of earlier years.

VII. The Influence of Puritanism on American Nomenclature.

Baptismal nomenclature to-day in the United States, especially in the old settlements, bears stronger impressions of the Puritan epoch than the English. Their ancestors were Puritans, who had fled England for conscience' sake. Their life, too, in the West was for generations primitive, almost patriarchal, in its simplicity. There was no bantering scorn of a wicked world to face; there was no deliberate effort made by any part of the community to restore the old names. To this day the impress remains. Take up a story of backwood life, such as American female writers affect so much, and it will be inscribed "Faith Gartney's Girlhood," or "Prudence Palfrey." All the children that figure in these tales are "Truth," or "Patience," or "Charity," or "Hope." The true descendants of the early settlers are, to a man, woman, and child, even now bearers of names either from the abstract Christian graces or the narratives of Holy Scripture. Of course, the constant tide of immigration that has set in has been gradually telling against Puritan traditions. The grotesque in name selection, too, has gone further in some of the more retired and inaccessible districts of the States than the eastern border, or in England generally, where social restraints and the demands of custom are still respected. If we are to believe American authorities, there are localities where humour has certainly become grim, and the solemn rite of baptism somewhat burlesqued by a selection of names which throw into the shade even Puritan eccentricity.

Look at the names of some of the earliest settlers of whom we have any authentic knowledge. We may mention the Mayflower first. In 1620 the emigrants by this vessel founded New Plymouth. This led to the planting of other colonies. Among the passengers were a girl named Desire Minter, a direct translation of Desiderata, which had just become popular in England; William Brewster, the ruling elder; his son Love Brewster, who married, settled, and died there in 1650, leaving four children; and a younger son, Wrestling Brewster. The daughters had evidently been left in England till a comfortable home could be found for them, for next year there arrived at New Plymouth, in the Ann and Little James, Fear Brewster and Patience Brewster. Patience very soon married Thomas Prince, one of the first governors. On this same memorable journey of the Mayflower came also Remember, daughter of Isaac Allerton, first assistant to the new governor; Resolved White, who married and left five children in the colony; and Humility Cooper, who by-and-by returned to England.

A little later on, in the Ann and Little James, again came Manasseh Faunce and Experience Mitchell. In a "List of Living" in Virginia, made February 16, 1623, is Peaceable Sherwood. In a "muster" taken January 30, 1624, occur Revolt Morcock and Amity Waine.

There is a conversation in "The Ordinary"—a drama written in 1634 or 1635, by Cartwright, the man whose "body was as handsome as his soul," as Langbaine has it—which may be quoted here. Hearsay says—

"London air,
Methinks, begins to be too hot for us.
Slicer. There is no longer tarrying here: let's swear
Fidelity to one another, and
So resolve for New England.
Hearsay. 'Tis but getting
A little pigeon-hole reformed ruff——
Slicer. Forcing our beards into th' orthodox bent——
Shape. Nosing a little treason 'gainst the king,
Bark something at the bishops, and we shall
Be easily received."
Act iv. sc. 5.

It is interesting to remember that 1635, when this was written, saw the high tide of Puritan emigration. The list of passengers that have come down to us prove it. After that date the names cease to represent the sterner spirit of revolt against episcopacy and the Star Chamber.

In the ship Francis, from Ipswich, April 30, 1634, came Just Houlding. In the Elizabeth, landed April 17, 1635, Hope-still Foster and Patience Foster. From the good barque James, July 13, 1635, set foot on shore Remembrance Tybbott. In the Hercules sailed hither, in 1634, Comfort Starre, "chirurgeon." In 1635 settled Patient White. In a book of entry, dated April 12, 1632, is registered Perseverance Greene, as one who is to be passed on to New England.

Such names as Constant Wood, Temperance Hall, Charity Hickman, Fayth Clearke, or Grace Newell, I simply record and pass on. That these names were perpetuated is clear. The older States teem with them now; American story-books for girls are full of them. Humility Cooper, of 1620, is met by an entry of burial in St. Michael's, Barbados:

"1678, May 16. Humility Hobbs, from ye almshous."

The churchwardens of St. James' Barbados, have entered an account of lands, December 20, 1679, wherein is set down

"Madam Joye Sparks, 12 servants, 150 negroes."

Increase Mather is a familiar name to students of American history. His father, Richard Mather, was born at Liverpool in 1596. Richard left for New England in 1635, with his four sons, Samuel, Nathaniel, Eleazar, and Increase. Cotton Mather was a grandson. About the same time, Charles Chauncey (of a Hertfordshire family), late Vicar of Ware, who had been imprisoned for refusing to rail in his communion table, settled in New England. Dying there in 1671, as president of Harvard College, he bequeathed, through his children, the following names to the land of his adoption:—Isaac, Ichabod, Sarah, Barnabas, Elnathan, and Nathaniel. Both the Mathers and the Chaunceys, therefore, sent out a Nathaniel. Adding these to the large number of Nathaniels found in the lists of emigrants published by Mr. Hotten, no wonder Nathaniel became for a time the first name on American soil, and that "Nat" should have got instituted into a pet name. Jonathan was not to be compared to it for a moment.

But we have not done with the Chaunceys. One of the most singular accidents that ever befell nomenclature has befallen them. What has happened to Sidney in England, has happened to Chauncey in America, only "more so." The younger Chaunceys married and begot children. A grandson of Isaac Chauncey died at Boston, in 1787, aged eighty-three. He was a great patriot, preacher, and philanthropist at a critical time in his country's history. The name had spread, too, and no wonder that it suggested itself to the authoress of "Uncle Tom's Cabin" as a character name. She, however, placed it in its proper position as a surname. It may be that Mrs. Stowe has given the use of this patronymic as a baptismal name an impulse, but it had been so used long before she herself was born. It was a memorial of Charles Chauncey, of Boston. It has now an average place throughout all the eastern border and the older settlements. I take up the New York Directory for 1878, and at once light upon Chauncey Clark, Chauncey Peck, and Chauncey Quintard; while, to distinguish the great Smith family, there are Chauncey Smith, lawyer, Chauncey Smith, milk-dealer, Chauncey Smith, meat-seller, and Chauncey Smith, junior, likewise engaged in the meat market. Thus, it is popular with all classes. In my London Directory for 1870, there are six Sidney Smiths and one Sydney Smith. Chauncey and Sidney seem likely to run a race in the two countries, but Chauncey has much the best of it at present.

Another circumstance contributed to the formation of Americanisms in nomenclature. The further the Puritan emigrants drew away from the old familiar shores, the more predominant the spirit of liberty grew. It was displayed, amongst other ways, in the names given to children born on board vessel. It was an outlet for their pent-up enthusiasm. Shakespeare puts into the mouth of Pericles—

"We cannot but obey
The powers above us. Could I rage and roar
As doth the sea she lies on, yet the end
Must be as 'tis. My gentle babe, Marina (whom,
For she was born at sea, I've named so) here
I charge your charity withal, leaving her
The infant of your care."
Act iii. sc. 3.

The Puritan did the same. Oceanus Hopkins was born on the high seas in the Mayflower, 1620; Peregrine White came into the world as the same vessel touched at Cape Cod; Sea-born Egginton, whose birth "happened in his berth," as Hood would say, is set down as owner of some land and a batch of negroes later on (Hotten, p. 453); while the marriage of Sea-mercy Adams with Mary Brett is recorded, in 1686, in Philadelphia (Watson's "Annals of Philadelphia," 1. 503). Again, we find the following:—

"1626, Nov. 6. Grant of denization to Bonaventure Browne, born beyond sea, but of English parents."—C. S. P.

No doubt his parents went over the Atlantic on board the Bonaventure, which was plying then betwixt England and the colonies (vide list of ships in Hotten's "Emigrants," pp. vii. and 35).

We have another instance in the "baptismes" of St. George's, Barbados:

"1678, Oct. 13. Samuel, ye son of Bonaventure Jellfes."

Allowing the father to be forty years old, his parents would be crossing the water about the time the good ship Bonaventure was plying.

Again, we find the following (Hotten, p. 245):—

"Muster of John Laydon:

"John Laydon, aged 44, in the Swan, 1606.

"Anne Laydon, aged 30, in the Mary Margett, 1608.

"Virginia Laydon (daughter), borne in Virginia."

All this, as will be readily conceived, has tended to give a marked character to New England nomenclature. The very names of the children born to these religious refugees are one of the most significant tokens to us in the nineteenth century of the sense of liberty they felt in the present, and of the oppression they had undergone in the past.

If we turn from these lists of passengers, found in the archives of English ports, not to mention "musters" already quoted, to records preserved by our Transatlantic cousins, we readily trace the effect of Puritanism on the first generation of native-born Americans.

From Mr. Bowditch's interesting book on "Suffolk Surnames," published in the United States, we find the following baptismal names to have been in circulation there: Standfast, Life, Increase, Supply, Donation, Deodat, Given, Free-grace, Experience, Temperance, Prudence, Mercy, Dependance, Deliverance, Hope, Reliance, Hopestill, Fearing, Welcome, Desire, Amity, Comfort, Rejoice, Pardon, Remember, Wealthy, and Consider. Nothing can be more interesting than the analysis of this list. With two exceptions, every name can be proved, from my own collection alone, to have been introduced from the mother country. In many instances, no doubt, Mr. Bowditch was referring to the same individual; in others to their children. The mention of Wealthy reminds us of Wealthy, Riches, and Fortune, already demonstrated to be popular English names. Fortune went out to New England in the person of Fortune Taylor, who appears in a roll of Virginian immigrants, 1623. Settling down there as a name of happy augury for the colonists' future, both spiritual and material, she reappears, in the person of Fortune the spinster, in the popular New England story entitled "The Wide, Wide World." Even "Preserved," known in England in 1640, was to be seen in the New York Directory in 1860; and Consider, which crossed the Atlantic two hundred and fifty years ago, so grew and multiplied as to be represented at this moment in the directory just mentioned, in the form of

"Consider Parish, merchant, Clinton, Brooklyn."

Mr. Bowditch adds "Search-the-Scriptures" to his list of names that crossed the Atlantic. This tallies with Search-the-Scriptures Moreton, of Salehurst, one of the supposed sham jury already treated of. He quotes also Hate-evil Nutter from a colonial record of 1649. Here again we are reminded of Bunyan's Diabolonian jury, one of whom was Hate-bad. It is all but certain from the date that Hate-evil went out from the old country. The name might be perfectly familiar to the great dreamer, therefore. Faint-not Wines, Mr. Bowditch says, became a freeman in 1644, so that the popularity of that great Puritan name was not allowed to be limited by the English coast. In this same year settled Faithful Rouse—one more memorial of English nonconformity.

English Puritanism must stand the guilty cause of much modern humour, not to say extravagance, in American name-giving. Puns compounded of baptismal name and surname are more popular there than with us. Robert New has his sons christened Nothing and Something. Price becomes Sterling Price; Carrol, Christmas Carrol; Mixer, Pepper Mixer; Hopper, Opportunity Hopper; Ware, China Ware; Peel, Lemon Peel; Codd, Salt Codd; and Gentle, Always Gentle. It used to be said of the English House of Commons that there were in it two Lemons, with only one Peel, and the Register-General not long since called attention in one of his reports to the existence of Christmas Day. We have, too, Cannon Ball, Dunn Brown, Friend Bottle (London Directory), and River Jordan, not to mention two brothers named Jolly Death and Sudden Death, the former of whom figured in a trial lately as witness. The Times of December 7, 1878, announced the death of Mr. Emperor Adrian, a Local Government Board member. Nevertheless, the practice prevails much more extensively across the water, and the reason is not far to seek.

Mr. Bowditch seems to imagine, we notice, America to be a modern girl's name. He says administration upon the estate of America Sparrow was granted in 1855, while in 1857 America C. Tabb was sued at law. America and Americus were in use in England four hundred years ago

(vide "English Surnames," 2nd edit., p. 29), and two centuries ago we meet with
"America Baguley, 1669, his halfpeny,"
on a token. Amery was the ordinary English dress.

EPILOGUE.

DOUBLE CHRISTIAN NAMES: THEIR RISE AND PROGRESS.

I. Royal Double Names.

"But two christian names are rare in England, and I only remember now his Majesty, who was named Charles James, as the Prince his sonne Henry Frederic: and among private men, Thomas Maria Wingfield and Sir Thomas Posthumus Hobby."—Camden.

If we take this sentence literally, the great antiquary, who knew more of the families and pedigrees of the English aristocracy than any other man of his day, could only recall to his mind four cases of double Christian names. This was in 1614.

At the outset, therefore, there is significance in this statement. Mr. Blunt, in his "Annotated Prayer-Book," says of "N. or M." in the Catechism—

"N. was anciently used as the initial of Nomen, and 'Nomen vel Nomina' was expressed by 'N. vel NN.,' the double N being afterwards corrupted into M."

If this be a correct explanation, "M." must refer to cases where more than one child was brought to the priest, N. standing for an occasion where only one infant was presented. In a word, "N. or M." could not stand for "Thomas or Thomas Henry," but for "Thomas or Thomas and Henry." If this be unsatisfactory, then Mr. Blunt's explanation is unsatisfactory.

Camden's sentence may be set side by side with Lord Coke's decision. In his "First Institute" (Coke upon Littleton) he says—

"And regularly it is requisite that the purchaser be named by the name of baptism, and his surname, and that special heed be taken to the name of baptism; for that a man cannot have two names of baptism, as he may have divers surnames."

Again, he adds—

"If a man be baptized by the name of Thomas, and after, at his confirmation by the bishop, he is named John, he may purchase by the name of his confirmation.... And this doth agree with our ancient books, where it is holden that a man may have divers names at divers times, but not divers christian names."

This is all very plain. Even in James I.'s days thousands of our countrymen had no fixed surnames, and changed them according to caprice or fancy. But the christian name was a fixture, saving in the one case of confirmation. Lord Coke is referring to an old rule laid down by Archbishop Peckham, wherein any child whose baptismal name, by accident or evil thought, had a bad significance is advised, if not compelled, to change it for one of more Christian import.

The chief point of interest, however, in this decision of Lord Coke's, is the patent fact that no thought of a double christian name is present in his mind. Had it been otherwise, he would never have worded it as he has done. Archbishop Peckham's rule had evidently been infringed, and Lord Coke upholds the infringement. A child with such an orthodox name as Thomas (a name with no immoral significance) might, he lays it down, become John at confirmation. Even in such a case as this, however, John is not to be added to Thomas; it must take its place, and Thomas cease to be recognized.

Lord Coke, of course, was aware that Charles I.'s queen was Henrietta Maria, the late king Charles James, and his son Henry Frederic. It is possible, nay probable, that he was not ignorant of Thomas Maria Wingfield's existence, or that of Thomas Posthumus Hobby. But that these double baptismal names should ever become an every-day custom, that the lower and middle classes should ever adopt them, that even the higher orders should ever go beyond the use of "Maria" and "Posthumus," seems never to have suggested itself to his imagination.

There is no doubt the custom came from France in the first instance. There, as in England, it was confined to the royal and aristocratic circles. The second son of Catharine de' Medici was baptized Edward Alexander in 1551. Mary Stuart followed the new fashion in the names of her son Charles James. The higher nobility of England slowly copied the practice, but within most carefully prescribed limits.

One limitation was, the double name must be one already patronized by royalty.

Henrietta Maria found her title repeated in Henrietta Maria Stanley, daughter of the ill-fated James, Earl of Derby, who for his determined loyalty was beheaded at Bolton, in Lancashire, in 1651. She was born on the 17th of November, 1630, and was buried in York Minster on the 13th of January, 1685. Sir Peter Ball, attorney to the queen of Charles I., baptized his seventeenth child by the name of his royal mistress, Henrietta Maria. He followed her fortunes after as before the king's execution (Polwhel's "Devon," p. 157). These must both have been considered remarkable cases in their day. The loyalty of the act would be its sanction in the eyes of their friends.

But while some copied the double name of the queen (also the name of the queen's mother), other nobles who had boys to christen mimicked the royal nursery of James I. Henry Frederick, Earl of Arundel, was born in 1608, and Henry Frederick Thynne, brother of Lord Weymouth, was created a baronet in 1641. No one need doubt the origin of these double forms. Again loyalty would be their answer against objections.

But side by side with these went "Maria" (used for either sex) and "Posthumus," or Posthuma—the only two instances recalled by Camden as in use among "private men." There seems good reason to believe that, for two or three generations at least, these were deemed, by some unwritten code, the only permissible second names outside the royal list.

The case of Wingfield is curious. Three generations, at least, bore a second name "Maria," all males. The first was Edward Maria, of Kimbolton, who received the female title in honour of, and from, the Princess Mary, daughter of Henry VIII., his godmother; the second was Thomas Maria, adduced by Camden; and the third is referred to in the following document:

"1639, April. Bill of complaint relative to the sale of the manor of Keyston, Hunts, by Edward Maria Wingfield."—C. S. P., 1639.

Maria had long been common in Italy, France, and Spain, as a second name, and still is, whether for a boy or girl, the child being thereby specially committed to the protection of the Virgin. The earliest instances in England, however, were directly given in honour of two royal godmothers, who happened to be Mary in one case, and Henrietta Maria in the other. Hence the seeming transference of the foreign second name Maria to our own shores. Thus introduced,

Maria began to circulate in society generally as an allowed second name:

"1610, July 10. Baptized Charles Maria, sonne of Charles Chute, Esquire."—St. Dunstan-in-the-West.

"1640, ——. Died Gulielma Maria Posthuma Springett."—Tablet, Ringmer, Lewes, Sussex.

This last was a bold procedure, three names being an unheard-of event. But the sponsor might reply that he was only placing together the two recognized second names, Maria and Posthuma. Later on, Maria is again found in the same family. In the year 1672, William Penn, the Quaker, married Gulielma Maria, daughter of Sir William Springett.

Posthuma (as in the above instance), or Posthumus, is still more remarkable. The idea of styling a child by this name, thus connecting its birth with the father's antecedent death, seems to have touched a sympathetic chord, and the practice began widely to prevail. The first example I have seen stands as a single name. Thus, in the Canterbury Cathedral register, is recorded:

"1572, Feb. 10. Christened Posthumus, the sonne of Robert Pownoll."

The following is the father's entry of burial:

"1571, June 8. Buried Robert Pownoll."

This is the earliest instance I have seen. Very soon it was deemed right to make it a second name:

"1632, Sept. 18. Baptized Henry Postumus, son of James Gamble."—Doncaster.

Sir Thomas Posthumus Hoby, Knight, lord of the manor of Hackness, died in 1641. He bequeathed the greater portion of his estates to "his dearly beloved and esteemed cozen John Sydenham," of Brimpton, Somerset, who, being baroneted in July, 1641, died in 1642, and was succeeded by his son Sir John Posthumus Sydenham. Posthumus, possibly, in this case was commemorative of Sir Thomas, and not of Sir John. William Ball, son of Sir Peter Ball, already mentioned, married Maria Posthuma Hussey. This must have occurred before the Commonwealth, but I have not the exact date.

The character of all these names is sufficient proof of their rarity. All belong, with one exception, to the higher ranks of society. All were called after the children in the royal nursery, or Maria or Posthuma was the second component. Several formed the double name with both. It seems certain that at first it was expected that, if people in high life were to give encouragement to the new fashion, they must do so within certain carefully defined limits. As for any lower class, it was never imagined that they would dream of aspiring to such a daring innovation. The earliest instance of this class, I find, still has Mary for its second component, and commemorates two English queens:

"1667, Jan. 12. Baptized Elizabeth Mary, being of the age of 18 and upwards, daughter to John Allen, and Emm his wife, both of them being pro-baptists."—Cant. Cath.

Even to the close of the seventeenth century, if a middle-class man gave his child a double name, it must be to commemorate royalty:

"1696, June 4. Baptized William Henry, son of Mr. Jacob Janeway, and Francis his wife."—Cant. Cath.

William III. was christened William Henry.

Speaking of Mary's husband, we may add that two of the most familiar conjunctions of the present day among the middle and lower classes, that of Anna Maria or Mary Ann, arose similarly. In Italy and France the two went together a hundred years earlier, in connection with the Virgin and her mother. In England they are only found since 1700, being used as commemorative of the sisters Anne and Mary, both queens. Like William Henry, the combination has been popular ever since:

"1717, Feb. 15. Christened Anne-Mary, d. of James Hebert, mercer.

"1729, March 30. Christened Anna-Maria, d. of Thomas and Mary Hoare, pewterer."—St. Dionis Backchurch.

The clerk of Finchley Church could not understand this conjunction—not to add that his education seems to have been slightly neglected:

"1715, Feb. 26. Baptized Anammeriah, d. of Thomas and Eliz. Biby.

"1716, Mch. 17. Baptized Anameriah, d. of Richard and Sarah Bell."

These are the first double names to be found in this register.

The Latin form represents the then prevailing fashion. There was not a girl's name in use that was not Latinized. Goldsmith took off the custom in his "Vicar of Wakefield," in the names of Sophia, Olivia, and Carolina Wilhelmina Amelia Skeggs. The latter hit at the new rage for double and treble baptismal names also; for the day came when two names were not enough. In 1738 George III. was christened George William Frederic. Gilly Williams, writing to George Selwyn, December 12, 1764, says—

"Lord Downe's child is to be christened this evening. The sponsors I know not, but his three names made me laugh not a little—John Christopher Burton. I wish to God, when he arrives at the years of puberty, he may marry Mary Josephina Antonietta Bentley."—"Memoirs of George Selwyn," by Jesse, quoted by Mr. Waters in "Parish Registers," p. 31.

I need scarcely add that three do not nearly satisfy the craving of many people in the nineteenth century, nor did they everybody in the eighteenth:

"1781, April 29. Bapt. Charles Caractacus Ostorius Maximilian Gustavus Adolphus, son of Charles Stone, tailor."—Burbage, Wilts.

In Beccles Church occurs the following:

"1804, Oct. 14. Bapt. Zaphnaphpaaneah Isaiah Obededom Nicodemus Francis Edward, son of Henry and Sarah Clarke."

Only Francis Edward could be got in the ordinary place, so the rest had to be furnished in a note at the foot of the page.

"On Oct. 8th, 1876, in the revision of the parliamentary list at Preston, a claimant appeared bearing the name of Thomas Hill Joseph Napoleon Horatio Bonaparte Swindlehurst Nelson. The vote was allowed, and the revising barrister ordered the full name to be inserted on the register."—Manchester Evening News, October 11, 1876.

II. Conjoined Names.

Returning to the first half of the seventeenth century, we find strong testimony of the rarity of these double names, and a feeling that there was something akin to illegality in their use, from our registers, wherein an attempt was made to glue two names together as one, without a hyphen or a second capital letter. Take the following, all registered within a generation or two of Camden's remark:

"1602, May 24. Baptized Fannasibilla, d. of Thomas Temple."—Sibbesdon, Leicestershire.

Here is a palpable attempt to unite Francis (Fanny) and Sybil.

"1648, Jan. 25. Baptized Aberycusgentylis, son of Richard Balthropp, gent."—Iver, Buckingham.

Here the father has been anxious to commemorate the great Oxford professor, the father of international law, Dr. Abericus Gentilis. He has avoided a breach of supposed national law by writing the two names in one.

"1614, Aprill 16. Buried Jockaminshaw Butler, wife of James Butler, potter, in Bishopsgate Street."—St. Peter, Cornhill.

The surname of "Shaw" has done service hundreds of times since then as a second baptismal name.

"1640, May 7. Baptized Johnamaria, ye son of Frances Ansloe, and Clare his wife."—Cant. Cath.

Here again is the inevitable Maria, but so inwoven with John, that Lord Coke's legal maxim could not touch the case. It is the same in the following example:—

"1632, ——. Married John Pell to Ithamaria, d. of Henry Reynolles, of London."—Lower, "Worthies of Sussex," p. 178.

One of the most strange samples of conjoined names is this:

"1595, April 3. Joane, whome we maye call Yorkkooppe, because she was ye basterd daughter, as yt is comonlye reported, of one John York and Anne Cooper."—Landbeach.

Here is a double conjunction; John and Anne forming Jo-ane, and York and Cooper, Yorkkooppe. The first is neat, the second clumsy: but, doubtless, the clerk who wielded the goose-quill deemed both a masterpiece of ingenuity.

The following is interesting:—

"1616, July 13, being Satterday, about half an hour before 10 of the clocke in the forenoon, was born the Lady Georgi-Anna, daughter to the Right Hon. Lady Frances, Countess of Exeter; and the same Ladie Georgi-Anna was baptized 30th July, 1616, being Tuesday, Queen Anne and the Earl of Worcester, Lord Privie Seal, being witnesses: and the Lorde Bishop of London administered the baptism."—Vide R. E. C. Waters, "Parish Registers." 1870.

III. Hyphened Names.

It will be noticed that so far the two names were both (saving in the case of Aberycusgentylis and Jockaminshaw) from the recognized list of baptismal names. About the reign of Anne the idea of a patronymic for a second name seems to have occurred. To meet the supposed legal exigencies the two names were simply hyphened. We will confine our instances to the register of Canterbury Cathedral:

"1721, Jan. 20. Baptized Howe-Lee, son of Lee Warner, Esquire, and Mary his wife.

"1728, July 4. Baptized Francis-Gunsby, son of Dr. William Ayerst, prebendary of this church.

"1746, Sep. 28. Baptized James-Smith, son of James Horne, and Mary his wife."

I need not say that at first these children bore the name in common parlance of Howe-Lee, or Francis-Gunsby, or James-Smith. The two were never separated, but treated as one name. To this day traces of this eighteenth-century habit are to be found. I know an old gentleman and his wife, people of the old school, dwelling somewhat out of the world, who address a child invariably by all its baptismal titles. The effect is very quaint. In all formal and legal processes the two or three names have to be employed, and clergymen who only recite the first in the marriage service, as I have heard some do, are in reality guilty of misdemeanour.

How odd all these contrivances to modern eyes! We take up a directory, and every other registration we look on is made up of three names. The poorer classes are even more particular than the aristocracy upon the point. The lady-help, describing her own superior merit, says—

"Do not think that we resemble
Betsy Jane or Mary Ann,
Women born in lowly cottage,
Bred for broom or frying-pan."

And yet, in forty-nine church registers out of fifty, throughout the length and breadth of England, there will not be found a single instance of a double christian name previous to the year 1700. Mr. Maskell has failed to find any instance in the register of All-Hallows, Barking, and the Harleian Society's publication of the registers of St. Peter, Cornhill, and St. Dionis Backchurch only confirms the assertion I have made.

Many stories have arisen upon these double names. A Mr. Gray, bearing the once familiar Christian name of Anketil, wanted the certificate of his baptism. The register was carefully searched—in vain; the neighbouring registers were as thoroughly scanned—in vain. Again the first register was referred to, and upon a closer investigation he was found entered as Ann Kettle Gray.

Not very long ago a child was brought to the font for baptism. "What name?" asked the parson. "John," was the reply. "Anything else?" "John honly," said the godparent, putting in an "h" where it was not needed. "John Honly, I baptize thee," etc., continued the clergyman, thus thrown off his guard. The child was entered with the double name.

In Gutch's "Geste of Robin Hode" (vol. i. p. 342) there is a curious note anent Maid Marian, wherein some French writers are rebuked for supposing Marian to be composed of Mary and Ann, and the statement is made that it is from Mariamne, the wife of Herod! Marian or Marion, of course, is the diminutive of Mary, the other pet form being Mariot. Nevertheless the great commonness of the double christian name Mary Ann is consequent on the idea that Marian is compounded of both.

In the registers of marriages at Halifax parish church (December 1, 1878) is the name of a witness, Charity H———. He—it was a he—is the third child of his parents, two sisters, Faith and Hope, having preceded him. His full baptismal name is "And Charity," and in his own marriage certificate his name is so written. In ordinary affairs he is content with Charity alone (Notes and Queries, August 16, 1879). This could not have happened previous to Queen Anne's reign. Acts-

Apostles Pegden's will was administered upon in 1865. His four elder brothers bore the four Evangelists' names. This, again, could not well have occurred before the eighteenth century was in. In Yorkshire directories one may see such entries as John Berry, and immediately below, Young John Berry. This represents a common pleasantry at the font among the "tykes," but is necessarily modern. Nor could "Sir Isaac" or "Sir Robert," as prænomens to "Newton" or "Peel," have been originated at any distant period.

IV. The Decay of Single Patronymics in Baptism.

The introduction of double baptismal names produced a revolution as immediate as it was unintentional. It put a stop to what bade fair to become a universal adoption of patronymics as single baptismal names. This practice took its rise about the year 1580. It became customary in highly placed families to christen the eldest son by the name of the landed estate to which he was heir. Especially was it common when the son succeeded to property through his mother; then the mother's surname was his Christian name. With the introduction of second baptismal names, this custom ceased, and the boy or girl, as the case might be, after a first orthodox name of Robert or Cecilia, received as a second the patronymic that before was given alone. Instead of Neville Clarke the name would be Charles Neville Clarke. From the year 1700, say, this has been a growing custom, and half our present list of treble names are thus formed.

The custom of giving patronymic names was, for a century at least, peculiar to England, and is still rare on the Continent. Camden notices the institution of the practice:

"Whereas in late yeares sirnames have beene given for christian names among us, and no where else in Christendome: although many dislike it, for that great inconvenience will ensue: neverthelesse it seemeth to procede from hearty goodwill and affection of the godfathers, to shew their love, or from a desire to continue and propagate their owne names to succeeding ages. And is in no wise to bee disliked, but rather approved in those which, matching with heires generall of worshipfull ancient families, have given those names to their heires, with a mindefull and thankfull regard of them, as we have now Pickering, Wotton, Grevill, Varney, Bassingburne, Gawdy, Calthorpe, Parker, Pecsal, Brocas, Fitz-Raulfe, Chamberlanie, who are the heires of Pickering, etc."—"Remaines," 1614.

Fuller says—

"Reader, I am confident an instance can hardly be produced of a surname made christian in England, save since the Reformation.... Since it hath been common."—"Worthies," i. 159, 160.

For two hundred years this custom had the widest popularity among the higher classes, and from some of our registers there are traces that the lower orders were about to adopt the practice. In the case of female heiresses the effect is odd. However, this was got over sometimes by giving a feminine termination:

"1660, Aug. 28. John Hendon, Knight, of Biddenden in Kent, and Northamtonia Haward, of Tandridge in Surrey, married."—Streatham, Surrey.

"1711, Jan. 3. Buried Jermyna, d. of Mr. Edward Tyson, gent."—St. Dionis Backchurch.

"1699, March 7. Nathaniel Parkhurst and Althamia Smith, of Kensington, married."

Althamia was daughter of Altham Smyth, barrister, son of Sir Thomas Smyth, of Hill Hall,

Essex (Chester's "Westminster Abbey," p. 173).

But more often they were without the feminine desinence:

"1639, Oct. 18. Buried Essex, daughter of Lord Paget."—Drayton (Lyson's "Middlesex," p. 42).

Will of John Wilmot, Earl of Rochester, 1680 (Doctors' Commons):

"Item: To my daughter Mallet, when shee shall have attained the like age of sixteen, the summe of foure thousand pounds."

The Countess of Rochester was Elizabeth, daughter and heir of John Mallet, Esq., of Enmore, Somerset.

"1699. Petition of Windebank Coote, widow, to the Lords of the Treasury, showing that her husband Lambert Coote was a favourite servant of King Charles II., and left her with a great charge of children."—"C. Treas. P.," 1697-1702.

"Tamworth, daughter of Sir Roger Martin, of Long Melford, married Thomas Rookwood (who was born Aug. 18, 1658)."—"Collect. et Top.," vol. ii. p. 145.

"1596, Nov. 21. Baptized Cartwright, daughter of Nicholas Porter."—Aston-sub-Edge, Gloucester.

"1634, April 18. Baptized Steward, daughter of Sir Thomas Stanley, Knight."—Stepney, London.

"1656, March 24. Douglas Sheffield, daughter of Sir John Sheffield."—"Lunacy Commissions and Inquisitions," Record Office.

"1709, Feb. 3. Tankerville Chamberlyne, spinster, daughter of Edward C."—Ditto.

"1601, Feb. Buryed Handforth, d. Thomas Davenport, a soldier in Ireland."—Stockport Parish Church.

"1610, July 24. Baptized Kenburrow, ye daughter of Dr. Masters, one of the worshipfull prebendaries."—Cant. Cath.

"1688, March 29. Baptized Tufton, daughter of the Rev. Dr. James Jefferys, one of the prebendarys of this church."—Cant. Cath.

Even down to the middle of last century the custom was not uncommonly practised:

"1763, Sep. 15. Thomas Steady, of Chartham, to Chesterton Harnett, of the precincts of this church, spinster, by licence."—Cant. Cath.

"1759, June 12. Honourable Chatwynd Trumbull, widow."—"Lunacy Commissions and Inquisitions."

As to the male heirs, we need not furnish illustrations; they would require too much room:

"Sir Humphry Winch, Solicitor-General to Queen Elizabeth, married Cicely Onslowe. His eldest son was Onslowe Winch."—"Collect. et Top.," vol. iii. p. 86.

"Woodrove Foljambe, born Jan. 25, 1648, son of Peter Foljambe. His mother was Jane Woodrove, of Hope, Derbyshire."—Ditto, p. 88.

How common the practice was becoming among the better-class families the Canterbury register shall show:

"1601, April 16. Baptized Nevile, the sonne of Edwarde Whitegrave.

"1614, Nov. 28. Baptized Tunstall, sonn of Mr. William Scott, the sonn-in-lawe to the worshipful Mr. Tunstall, prebendary of this church.

"1615, May 15. Baptized Dudly, sonn of Mr. Doctor Jacksonn.

"1619, Dec. 16. Baptized Dudley, sonne of Sir John Wiles.

"1624, July 26. Baptized Sydney, sonne of Sirre William Barnes, Kt."

Dudley was, perhaps, the first surname that obtained a place among ordinary baptismal names:

"1614, Aug. 17. Christened Dudley, son of Thomas Styles.

"1684, April 17. Christened Dudley, son of Francis and Sarah Dylate."—St. Dionis Backchurch.

The introduction of surnames at the font permitted private predilections full play. At Canterbury we naturally find:

"1727, Feb. 22. Buried Cranmer Herris, gent., in ye cloisters."—Cant. Cath.

"1626, Oct. Baptized Bradford, sonne of Christopher Wilson, of Limehouse."—Stepney.

Hanover Stirling was a scholar of Trinity College, Dublin, in 1729. A Scotch Jacobite in London showed some skill in the heat of the great crisis of 1715:

"1715, June 10. Christened Margaret Jacobina, d. of Mr. Archiball Johnson, merchant."—St. Dionis Backchurch.

This will be sufficient. The custom is by no means extinct; but, through the introduction of second baptismal names, the practice is now rare, and all but entirely confined to boys. Two hundred and fifty years ago, it was quite as popular with the other sex.

Both Dudley and Sydney, mentioned above, have been used so frequently that they have now taken a place in our ordinary list of baptismal names. So far as Sydney is concerned, the reason is easily explained. The Smith family have been so fond of commemorating the great Sydney, that it has spread to other families. Chauncey and Washington occupy the same position in the United States.

V. The Influence of Foundling Names upon Double Baptismal Names.

One circumstance that contributed to the adoption of two baptismal names was the christening of foundlings. Having no father or mother to attest their parentage, being literally anonymous, there sprang up a custom, about the year 1500, of baptizing these children with a double title; only the second one was supposed to be the surname, and not a baptismal name at all. This second name was always a local name, betokening the precise spot, street, or parish where the child was found. Every old register has its numerous instances. The foundlings of St. Lawrence Jewry got the baptismal surname of Lawrence. At All-Hallows, Barking, the entries run:

"A child, out of Priest's Alley, christened Thomas Barkin.

"Christened a child out of Seething Lane, named Charles Parish.

"A child found in Mark Lane, and christened Mark Lane."—Maskell, "All-Hallows, Barking," p. 62.

At St. Dunstan-in-the-West they are still more diversified:

"1597, Mch. 1. Renold Falcon, a childe borne in Falcon Court, bapt.

"1611, May 11. Harbotles Harte, a poor childe found at Hart's dore in Fewter Lane, bapt.

"1614, March 26. Moses Dunstan, a foundlinge in St. Dunstan's hall, bapt.

"1618, Jan. 18. Mary Porch, a foundeling, bapt.

"1625, Aug. 7. Roger Middlesex was baptized.

"1627, May 19. Katherine Whitefryers was baptized."

"1610, Nov. Bapt. Elizabeth Christabell, d. of Alice Pennye, begotten in fornacacion."—Stepney, London.

"1586, May 21. Christening of Peter Grace, sonne of Katherine Davis, an harlot."—St. Peter, Cornhill.

"1592, Aug. 2. Christening of Roger Peeter, so named of our church; the mother a rogue, the childe was born the 22d July at Mr. Lecroft's dore."—Ditto.

The baptismal register of St. Dionis Backchurch teems with Dennis, or Dionys, as the name is entered:

"1623, Aug. 6. Joane Dennis, being laid at Mr. John Parke's doore in Fanchurch Streete.

"1627, June 3. Denis the Bastard, who was laid in the parish.

"1691, Nov. 19. Ingram Dionis, a fondling taken up in Ingram's Court."

We see in these registers the origin of the phrase, "It can't be laid at my door." Doubtless it was not always pleasant to have a little babe, however helpless, discovered on the doorstep. The gossips would have their "nods, and becks, and wreathed smiles," if they said nothing upon the subject. It was a common dodge to leave it on a well-known man's premises:

"1585, April 23. A man child was laid at Sir Edward Osbourne gate, and was named Dennis Philpot, and so brought to Christes Ospitall."

The same practice prevails in America. A New York correspondent wrote to me the other day as follows:—

"One babe, who was found in the vestibule of the City Hall, in this city (New York), was called John City Hall; another, Thomas Fulton, was found in Fulton Street in an ash-box; and a third, a fine boy of about four months, was left in the porch of Christ Church Rectory in Brooklyn. He was baptized by the name of Parish Church, by the Rev. Dr. Canfeild, the then rector."

The baptisms of "blackamoors" gave a double christian name, although the second was counted as a surname:

"Baptized, 1695, Mch. 27, John Wearmouth, a Tawny, taken captive, aged 20."—Bishop Wearmouth (Burns).

"Baptized, 1602-3, March, Christian Ethiopia, borne a Blackmore."—Stepney.

"Baptized, 1603, July, Charity Lucanoa, a Blackamor from Ratcliff."—Ditto.

"1744, Sep. 27. Rum John Pritchard, a Indian and Mahomitan, baptized this day by self at Mr. Pritchard's."—Fleet Registers (Burns).

"1717, ——. Baptized Charles Mustava, a black boy, servant to The Honble. Lord Hartford."—Preshute, Wilts.

Our forefathers did not seem to perceive it, but in all these cases double baptismal names were given. It must, however, have had its unfelt influence in leading up to the new custom, and especially to patronymics as second names. We are all now familiarized to these double and treble names. The poorest and the most abject creatures that bring a child to the font will have their string of grand and high-sounding titles; sometimes such a mouthful, that the parson's wonder is excited whence they accumulated them, till wonder is lost in apprehension lest he should fail to deliver himself of them correctly. The difficulty is increased when the name is pronounced as the fancy or education of the sponsor dictates. When one of three names is "Hugginy," the minister may be excused if he fails to understand all at once that "Eugénie" is intended. Such an incident occurred about six years ago, and the flustered parson, on a second inquiry, was not helped by the woman's rejoinder: "Yes, Hugginy; the way ladies does their 'air, you know."

We must confess we are not anxious to see the new custom—for new it is in reality—spread; but we fear much it will do so. We have reached the stage when three baptismal names are almost as common as two; and we cannot but foresee, if this goes on, that, before the century is out, our present vestry-books will be compelled to have the space allotted to the font names enlarged. As it is, the parson is often at his wits' end how to set it down.

Agnes, ,
Aholiab, ,
Aid-on-high,
Alathea,
Alianora,
Alice,
Aliot,
Alison,
Alpheus,
Altham,
Althamia,
Althea,
Always,
Alydea,
Amalasiontha,
Amelia,
America,
Americus,
Amery, ,
Amice,
Aminadab,
Amity, ,
Amor,
Amos, ,
Anammeriah,
Ananias, , , ,
And Charity,
Angel, ,
Angela,
Anger,
Anketill, ,
Anna, , ,
Anna Maria, ,
Anne, ,
Anne-Mary,
Annette,
Annora,
Annot, , , ,
Anot,
Antipas, ,

.

Antony,
Aphora,
Aphra,
Aphrah,
Appoline,
Aquila, ,
Araunah,
Arise, ,
Asa,
Ashael,
Ashes, ,
Assurance,
Atcock,
Atkin,
Atkinson,
Audria,
Austen,
Austin,
Avery, ,
Avice,
Awdry, ,
Axar,
Aymot,
Azariah,
Azarias, ,
B
Bab, ,
Badcock,
Baldwin, ,
Baptist,
Barbara, ,
Barbelot,
Barijirehah,
Barjonah,
Barnabas, ,
Barrabas,
Bartholomew, , , , , , , ,
Bartelot, ,
Bartle,
Bartlett,

Barzillai,
Bat, , , ,
Batcock, , , ,
Bate, , , ,
Bathsheba, ,
Bathshira,
Bathshua,
Batkin, , , ,
Battalion,
Batty,
Bawcock,
Beata, , ,
Beatrice,
Beatrix, ,
Beelzebub,
Belief,
Beloved,
Ben,
Benaiah,
Benedict,
Benedicta, ,
Bennet,
Benjamin,
Benoni,
Bess, , ,
Bessie, ,
Be-steadfast,
Be-strong,
Betha,
Be-thankful, ,
Bethia,
Bethsaida,
Bethshua,
Beton,
Betsy,
Bett,
Betty, , ,
Beulah,
Bezaleel,
Bill,

Blaze, ,
Boaz,
Bob, ,
Bodkin,
Bonaventure,
Bradford,
Bride,
Brownjohn,
C
Cain,
Caleb, , , ,
Canaan,
Cannon,
Caroletta,
Carolina, ,
Carolina Wilhelmina Amelia, ,
Caroline,
Cartwright,
Cassandra,
Catharine, , , ,
Cecilia, , , , , , , , , ,
Centurian,
Cess,
Cesselot,
Changed,
Charity, , , , , , , , ,
Charity Lucanoa,
Charles, ,
Charles Caractacus Ostorius Maximilian Gustavus Adolphus,
Charles James, ,
Charles Maria,
Charles Mustava,
Charles Neville,
Charles Parish,
Charlotte,
Chatwynd,
Chauncey, , ,
Cherubin,
Chesterton,
China,

Christ,
Christian, , ,
Christiana,
Christian Ethiopia,
Christmas,
Christopher,
Christophilus,
Church-reform,
Chylde-of-God,
Cibell,
Cissot,
Clarice,
Clemence,
Clemency,
Cloe,
Cock,
Col,
Cole, , ,
Colet,
Colin, , ,
Colinet, ,
Coll,
Collet,
Collin,
Colling,
Collinge,
Comfort, , , ,
Con, , ,
Confidence,
Consider, ,
Constance,
Constancy, ,
Constant, , , ,
Continent, ,
Cornelius,
Cotton,
Cranmer,
Creatura Christi,
Creature, ,
Cressens,

Crestolot,
Cuss,
Cussot, ,
Cust, ,
Custance, ,
D
Dalilah,
Damaris, , ,
Dameris, ,
Dammeris,
Dammy,
Dampris,
Damris,
Dancell-Dallphebo-Marke-Antony-Dallery-Gallery-Cesar,
Daniel, ,
Dankin,
Dannet,
Darcas,
David,
Daw,
Dawkin,
Dawks,
Dean,
Deb, ,
Deborah, , , ,
Deccon,
Degory,
Deliverance, , ,
Delivery,
Dennis, ,
Dennis Philpot,
Deodat,
Deodatus,
Deonata,
Depend,
Dependance,
Desiderata, ,
Desiderius,
Desire, , ,
Diccon, ,

Dicconson,
Dick, , , , ,
Dickens, ,
Dickenson, ,
Dickin, ,
Die-well,
Diffidence,
Diggon,
Digory,
Diligence,
Dinah, , , ,
Dionisia, ,
Dionys,
Diot,
Discipline,
Discretion,
Dobbin,
Dobinet, , ,
Do-good, ,
Dogory,
Doll, , , , ,
Dolly, ,
Donate,
Donation,
Donatus, ,
Dora,
Dorcas, , , ,
Do-right,
Dorothea, ,
Dorothy, , ,
Douce, ,
Doucet,
Douglas,
Dowcett,
Do-well,
Dowsabel,
Dowse,
Dowsett,
Drew, , ,
Drewcock,

Drewet, ,
Drocock,
Drusilla,
Dudley, ,
Duke,
Dun,
Dunn,
Dust, ,
E
Earl,
Easter, ,
Ebbot,
Ebed-meleck, , ,
Ebenezer,
Eden,
Edward Alexander,
Edward Maria,
Elcock,
Eleanor,
Eleanora,
Eleazar,
Elena, ,
Eleph,
Eliakim,
Elias, , ,
Elicot,
Elihu,
Eli-lama-Sabachthani,
Eliot,
Elisha,
Elisot,
Eliza, ,
Elizabeth, ,
Elizabeth Christabell,
Elizabeth Mary,
Elizar,
Elkanah,
Ellice, ,
Ellicot,
Elliot,

Ellis, , ,
Ellisot,
Elnathan, ,
Emanuel, , , ,
Emery,
Emm, ,
Emma, , , , , , ,
Emmett,
Emmot, , , , , ,
Emmotson,
Emperor,
Enecha,
Enoch,
Enot,
Epaphroditus, ,
Epenetus, ,
Ephin,
Ephraim, ,
Epiphany, ,
Er,
Erasmus,
Erastus, ,
Esaias, ,
Esau,
Esaye,
Essex,
Esther, ,
Eugénie,
Eunice,
Euodias,
Eve, ,
Evett,
Evot,
Evott,
Experience, , , , ,
Ezechell,
Ezeckiell,
Ezekias,
Ezekiel, , ,
Ezekyell,

Ezot,
Ezota,
F
Faint-not, , , , ,
Faith, , , , , , , ,
Faithful, , ,
Faith-my-joy,
Fannasibilla,
Fare-well, ,
Fauconnet,
Fawcett,
Fear,
Fear-God, , ,
Fearing,
Fear-not, ,
Fear-the-Lord,
Feleaman,
Felicity,
Fick,
Ficken,
Figg,
Figgess,
Figgin,
Figgins,
Figgs,
Fight-the-good-fight-of-faith, , ,
Flie-fornication, , ,
Forsaken,
Fortune, ,
Francis,
Francis-Gunsby,
Frank, ,
Free-gift, , ,
Free-grace,
Free-man, ,
Frideswide,
Friend,
From-above, ,
Fulk, ,
Fulke,

G
Gabriel, , ,
Gamaliel, ,
Gavin,
Gawain,
Gawen,
Gawin, ,
Gawyn, ,
Geoffrey,
George, , ,
George William Frederic,
Georgi-Anna,
Georgina,
Gercyon,
Gershom, , ,
Gersome,
Gertrude,
Gervase,
Gib,
Gibb,
Gibbet,
Gibbin,
Gibbing,
Gibbon,
Gilbert,
Gill, ,
Gillian, ,
Gillot,
Gillotyne,
Gilpin,
Given, ,
Give-thanks,
Goddard,
Godgivu,
God-help,
Godly, ,
Godric,
Goliath,
Good-gift,
Good-work,

Grace, , , , , ,
Graceless,
Gracious, ,
Grigg,
Grissel,
Grizill,
Guion,
Guiot,
Guillotin,
Gulielma Maria,
Gulielma Maria Posthuma,
Guy, , , ,
Gyllian,
H
Habakkuk,
Hadassah,
Hal,
Halkin,
Hallet,
Hamelot,
Hameth,
Hamilton,
Hamlet, , , , , , ,
Hammett,
Hamnet, , ,
Hamon, , ,
Hamond, , , ,
Hamonet,
Hamynet,
Han-cock, ,
Handcock,
Handforth,
Handmaid, ,
Hankin, , ,
Hanna,
Hannah, , ,
Hanover,
Harbotles Harte,
Hariph,
Harriet,

Harriot,
Harry, , , ,
Hate-bad, ,
Hate-evil, , , ,
Hatill,
Have-mercie,
Hawkes,
Hawkin,
Hawkins,
Hawks,
Heacock,
Heavenly-mind,
Heber,
Helpless,
Help-on-high, , , ,
Henrietta Maria, , ,
Henry, , , ,
Henry Frederick, ,
Henry Postumus,
Hephzibah,
Hercules,
Hester, ,
Hew,
Hewet, ,
Hewlett,
Hick, ,
Hickin,
Higg,
Higget,
Higgin, , ,
Higgot, ,
Hillary,
Hiscock,
Hitch-cock,
Hobb,
Hobelot,
Hodge, , ,
Hold-the-world,
Honest,
Honora, ,

Honour, , ,
Hope, , , , , ,
Hopeful, , ,
Hope-on-high,
Hope-still, , , ,
Hope-well,
Hopkin,
Hopkins,
Howe-Lee,
Hud,
Huelot,
Huggin,
Huggins,
Hugginy,
Hugh, , , , ,
Hughelot,
Hugonet, ,
Huguenin,
Huguenot,
Hugyn,
Humanity,
Humble, ,
Humiliation,
Humility, , ,
Humphrey,
Hutchin,
Hutchinson,
Hyppolitus,
I
Ibbetson,
Ibbett,
Ibbot, ,
Ibbotson,
Ichabod, ,
If-Christ-had-not-died-for-thee-thou-hadst-been-damned,
Immanuel,
Increase, , , , ,
Increased, , ,
Ingram,
Ingram Dionis,

Inward,
Isaac, , , , , ,
Isabella, , , , ,
Isaiah,
Issott,
Ithamaria,
J
Jabez,
Jachin,
Jack, , , , ,
Jackcock,
Jackett,
Jacob,
Jacolin,
Jacomyn, ,
Jacquinot,
Jaell, ,
James,
James-Smith,
Jane, , ,
Jannet,
Jannetin,
Janniting,
Jannotin,
Japhet,
Jeduthan,
Jeffcock, , ,
Jeffkin,
Jehoiada,
Jehostiaphat,
Jenkin, , ,
Jenkinson,
Jenks,
Jennin,
Jenning, ,
Jeremiah, , ,
Jeremy, , , ,
Jermyna,
Jerry,
Jesus-Christ-came-into-the-world-to-save,

Jethro,
Jill, , ,
Joab,
Joan, ,
Joane Dennis,
Joane Yorkkoope,
Job, , ,
Job-rakt-out-of-the-asshes, ,
Joel,
Jockaminshaw, ,
John, , , , , , , , , , , ,
Johnamaria,
John Christopher Burton,
John City Hall,
Johncock,
John Posthumus,
John Wearmouth,
Jolly,
Jonadab,
Jonathan, ,
Jordan, , ,
Jordanson,
Joseph,
Joshua,
Joskin,
Jowett,
Joy-againe,
Joyce, , , ,
Joye,
Joy-in-sorrow,
Juckes,
Juckin,
Judas,
Judas-not-Iscariot,
Judd, , ,
Jude,
Judith, , ,
Judkin, ,
Judson,
Jukes,

Julian,
Juliana,
Juliet,
Junior,
Just,
Justice,
K
Kate, , ,
Katherine Whitefryers,
Kelita,
Kenburrow,
Kerenhappuch,
Keturah,
Keziah,
Kit, ,
Knowledge,
L
Lætitia, ,
Lais, ,
Lambert,
Lamberton,
Lambin, ,
Lambinet,
Lambkin,
Lamblin,
Lament, , ,
Lamentation, ,
Lamentations,
Lamin,
Laming,
Lammin,
Lamming,
Lampin,
Lampkin,
Larkin, ,
Lawrence,
Laycock,
Leah, , ,
Learn-wisdom,
Learn-wysdome,

Lemon,
Lemuel,
Lesot,
Lettice, , ,
Life,
Lina,
Linot,
Little,
Littlejohn,
Live-loose,
Lively,
Live-well, ,
Living,
Louisa,
Love, , ,
Love-God, , ,
Love-lust,
Love Venus,
Love-well,
Luccock,
M
Mab,
Mabbott,
Mabel,
Madge, ,
Magdalen,
Magnify,
Magot,
Mahaliel,
Mahershalalhashbaz, , ,
Major,
Makin,
Makinson,
Malachi, , ,
Malkin, , ,
Malkynson,
Mallet,
Manasseh, ,
Margaret, ,
Margaret Jacobina,

Margerie, ,
Margett,
Margotin,
Margott,
Maria, , , ,
Marian, ,
Maria Posthuma,
Marion, ,
Mariot,
Mariotin,
Marioton,
Mark Lane,
Marshall,
Martha,
Mary, , , , , ,
Mary Ann, ,
Mary Given,
Mary Josephina Antonietta,
Mary Porch,
Mat, ,
Matathias,
Mathea,
Matilda, , , , ,
Matthew, , ,
Maud, ,
Maurice,
Maycock, ,
Meacock,
Meakin,
Mehetabell,
Melchisedek, , , ,
Melior,
Mephibosheth,
Mercy, , , , ,
Meshach, ,
Michael, ,
Michalaliel,
Micklejohn,
Milcom,
Miles, ,

Miracle,
Mocock,
Mokock,
Moll, ,
Mordecai, ,
Mordecay,
More-fruite, , , ,
Morrice,
Moses Dunstan,
Much-mercy, , ,
Mun,
Mycock,
My-sake,
N
Nab, ,
Nan, , , ,
Nancy, ,
Naphtali,
Nat, ,
Nathaniel, , , , , , ,
Natkin,
Nazareth,
Ned,
Nehemiah, ,
Nell,
Neptune,
Neriah,
Neville, ,
Nichol,
Nicholas, , , , , , , , , , ,
Nick,
Noah, , ,
Noel, , ,
No-merit, , ,
Northamtonia,
Nothing,
Nowell, ,
O
Obadiah,
Obediah, , ,

Obedience,
Obey,
Oceanus,
Olive,
Olivia, , ,
Onesiphorus, , ,
Onslowe,
Opportunity,
Original, ,
Othniell,
Oziell,
P
Palcock,
Pardon,
Paris,
Parish Church,
Parkin,
Parnel,
Parratt,
Pascal,
Pasche,
Pascoe,
Pash,
Pashkin,
Pask, ,
Paskin,
Patience, , , , , , ,
Patient,
Paul,
Payn,
Paynet,
Paynot,
Peaceable,
Peacock, ,
Peg,
Pelatiah,
Peleg,
Pentecost, , ,
Pepper,
Peregrine,

Perkin, ,
Perks,
Perot,
Perrin, , , ,
Perrinot,
Perrot, ,
Perrotin,
Perseverance, , ,
Persis, ,
Peter, , , , , , , , , ,
Peter Grace,
Petronilla,
Pharaoh, , ,
Phebe,
Philadelphia,
Philcock,
Philemon, , ,
Philip, , , , , , , , , ,
Philiponet,
Phillis,
Philpot, , ,
Phineas,
Phippin, ,
Phip, ,
Pidcock,
Pierce,
Pierre,
Piers,
Piety,
Pipkin,
Pleasant,
Pol,
Pontius Pilate,
Posthuma, ,
Posthumus, , , , ,
Potkin,
Praise-God, , , ,
Presela,
Preserved, ,
Prince,

Pris,
Priscilla, , , ,
Properjohn,
Providence,
Pru, ,
Prudence, , , , , , ,
Prudentia, ,
Purifie,
Purkiss,
Q
Quod-vult-Deus,
R
Rachel, , , ,
Ralph, , , ,
Ramoth-Gilead,
Raoul,
Raoulin,
Rawlings,
Rawlins,
Rawlinson,
Rebecca, , ,
Redeemed, ,
Redemptus,
Rediviva,
Reformation,
Refrayne,
Rejoice, , , ,
Rejoyce,
Reliance,
Relictus,
Remember, ,
Remembrance,
Renata,
Renatus, ,
Renewed, , ,
Renold Falcon,
Renovata, ,
Repent, , ,
Repentance, , , , , ,
Replenish,

See-truth,
Sehon,
Selah, ,
Senchia,
Sense, ,
Seraphim,
Seth, ,
Seuce,
Shadrach, ,
Shadrack,
Shallum, ,
Shelah,
Shorter,
Sib, , ,
Sibb,
Sibby,
Sibilla,
Sibot,
Sibyl,
Sidney,
Silcock,
Silence, , , ,
Silkin,
Sill, , , ,
Sim, , ,
Simcock, ,
Simkin,
Simon, , , , , , ,
Simpkinson,
Sincere,
Sin-denie,
Sin-deny,
Sir Isaac, ,
Sir Robert, ,
Sirs,
Sis, , ,
Sissot, ,
Something,
Sophia, , ,
Sorry-for-sin, ,

Sou'wester,
Squire,
Standfast, ,
Stand-fast-on-high,
Stedfast,
Stepkin,
Sterling,
Steward,
Subpena,
Sudden,
Supply,
Susan, , , ,
Susanna,
Susey,
Sybil, ,
Sydney, , , ,
Syssot,
T
Tabitha, ,
Tace, ,
Tacey,
Talitha-Cumi,
Talkative,
Tamar, , , ,
Tamaris,
Tamsin,
Tamson,
Tamworth,
Tankerville,
Tebbutt,
Tellno,
Temperance, , , , , , ,
Tetsy,
Tetty,
Thank,
Thankful, , , , ,
Thanks, ,
Theobald, , ,
Theobalda,
Theophania,

Theophilus, ,
Tholy,
Thomas, , , , , , , , ,
Thomas Barkin,
Thomasena,
Thomaset,
Thomas Fulton,
Thomas Hill Joseph Napoleon Horatio Bonaparte Swindlehurst Nelson,
Thomasin,
Thomasine, ,
Thomas Maria,
Thomas Posthumus, ,
Thomazin,
Thomesin,
Thurstan,
Thurston,
Tib, , , , ,
Tibbe, ,
Tibbett,
Tibbin,
Tibbitt,
Tibet, , ,
Tibbot,
Tibot, ,
Tiffanie,
Tiffany, ,
Tiffeny,
Tillett,
Tillot,
Tillotson,
Tim,
Timothy,
Tipkin,
Tippin,
Tipping,
Tippitt,
Tobel,
Toll,
Tollett,
Tollitt,

Tolly, ,
Tom, , , , , , , , ,
Tomasin,
Tomkin, ,
Tonkin,
Trial,
Tribulation, , , ,
Trinity,
True-heart,
Truth, , ,
Tryphena, ,
Tryphosa, ,
Tufton,
Tunstall,
Tyffanie,
Tyllot,
Typhenie,
U
Unfeigned,
Unity,
Upright,
Urias,
Ursula, ,
V
Vashni,
Venus, , , ,
Victory,
Virginia,
Virtue,
Vitalis, ,
W
Walter,
Warin,
Warinot,
Washington,
Wat, , ,
Watchful,
Watkin, , , ,
Watkins,
Watt,

Weakly,
Wealthy, , ,
Welcome,
What-God-will,
Wilcock, , , ,
Wilkin, , , ,
Will, , , ,
Willan,
William, , , , , , , , ,
William Henry,
Willin,
Willing,
Willot,
Wilmot, , , ,
Windebank,
Woodrove,
Wrath,
Wrestling,
Wyatt, ,
Wyon,
Y
Young Allen,
Young John, ,
Z
Zabulon,
Zachary, , ,
Zanchy,
Zaphnaphpaaneah,
Zaphnaphpaaneah Isaiah Obededom Nicodemus Francis Edward,
Zeal-for-God,
Zeal-of-the-land, , , ,
Zebulon,
Zephaniah, ,
Zerrubabel, , , ,
Zillah,
Zipporah, ,

Printed by William Clowes and Sons, Limited, London and Beccles.

Footnotes:

This is easily proved. In the wardrobe accounts for Edward IV., 1480, occur the following items:—

"John Poyntmaker, for pointing of xl. dozen points of silk pointed with agelettes of laton."

"John Carter, for cariage away of a grete loode of robeux that was left in the strete."

"To a laborer called Rychard Gardyner working in the gardyne."

"To Alice Shapster for making and washing of xxiiii. sherts, and xxiiii. stomachers."

Shapster is a feminine form of Shapper or Shaper—one who shaped or cut out cloths for garments. All these several individuals, having no particular surname, took or received one from the occupation they temporarily followed.—"Privy Purse Expenses, Eliz. of York," p. 122.

Any number of such instances might be recorded. Mr. W. C. Leighton, in Notes and Queries, February 23, 1861, notices a deed dated 1347, wherein two John de Leightons, brothers, occur. Mr. Waters, in his interesting pamphlet, "Parish Registers" (p. 30), says that Protector Somerset had three sons christened Edward, born respectively 1529, 1539, and 1548. All were living at the same time. He adds that John Leland, the antiquary, had a brother John, and that John White, Bishop of Winchester 1556-1560, was brother to Sir John White, Knight, Lord Mayor in 1563.

"I also give to the said Robert ... that land which Hobbekin de Bothum held of me."—Ext. deed of Sir Robert de Stokeport, Knight, 1189-1199: Earwaker's "East Cheshire," p. 334.

I have seen Stepkin as a surname but once. Lieutenant Charles Stepkin served under the Duke of Northumberland, in 1640.—Peacock's "Army List of Roundheads and Cavaliers," p. 78.

Adekyn was the simple and only title of the harper to Prince Edward in 1306, who attended the cour plenière held by King Edward at the feast of Whitsuntide at Westminster.—Chappell, "Popular Music of ye Olden Time," p. 29.

Sill was the nick form of Sybil and Silas till the seventeenth century, when the Puritan Silence seized it. I have only seen one instance of the surname, "John Silkin" being set down as dwelling in Tattenhall, Cheshire, in 1531 (Earwaker's "East Cheshire," p. 56).

Nevertheless the surname did exist in Yorkshire in Richard II.'s reign:

"Willelmus Malkynson, and Dionisia uxor ejus, iiiid."—W. D. S.

I need not quote, in proof of the popularity of kin, our surnames of Simpkinson, Hopkins, Dickens, Dickenson, Watkins, Hawkins, Jenkinson, Atkinson, and the rest. I merely mention that the patronymics ending in kins got abbreviated into kiss, and kes, and ks. Hence the origin of our Perkes, Purkiss, Hawkes, and Hawks, Dawks, Jenks, Juckes, and Jukes (Judkins).

In this class we must assuredly place Figgins. In the Hundred Rolls appears "Ralph, son of Fulchon." Here, of course, is the diminutive of the once common Fulke. Fick and Figg were the nick forms:

"1 Henry VIII. To Fygge the taborer, 6d."—Churchwarden's Books of Kingston-on-Thames, Brand's "Pop. Ant.," i. 147.

The London Directory has all the forms and corruptions as surnames, including Fick, Ficken, Figg, Figgs, Figgess, and Figgins.

Guion was not half so popular in England as Guiot. There are fifty-five Wyatts to three Wyons in the London Directory (1870). If Spenser had written of Guyon two centuries earlier, this might have been altered. Guy Fawkes ruined Guy. He can never be so popular again.

Cornwall would naturally be last to be touched by the Reformation. Hence these old forms were still used to the close of Elizabeth's reign, as for instance:

"1576, March 24. Baptized Ibbett, d. of Kateryne Collys, bastard.

"1576, July 30. Baptized Isott, d. of Richard Moyle."—St. Columb Major.

This connection of Scripture name with present circumstance ran out its full period. In the diary of Samuel Jeake, a well-known Puritan of Rye, occurs this reference to his son, born August 13, 1688: "At 49 minutes past 11 p.m. exactly (allowing 10' that the sun sets at Rye before he comes to the level of the horizon, for the watch was set by the sun-setting), my wife was safely delivered of a son, whom I named Manasseh, hoping that God had now made me forget all my toils."—"History of Town and Port of Rye," p. 576. Manasseh = forgetfulness.

A bishop may be instanced. Aylmer, who succeeded Sandys in the see of London, was for many years a favourer of Puritanism, and had been one of the exiles. His sixth son was Tobel (i.e. God is good), of Writtle, in Essex. Archbishop Whitgift was his godfather, and the reason for his singular appellation was his mother's being overturned in a coach without injury when she was pregnant (Cooper's "Ath. Cant." ii. 172).

Again: "At Dr. Whitaker's death, his wife is described as being 'partui vicina,' and a week afterwards her child was christened by the name of Jabez, doubtless for the scriptural reason 'because, she said, I bare him with sorrow.'"—Cooper's "Ath. Cant." ii. 197.

Esther's other name of Hadassah had a share of favour. So late as William and Mary's reign we find the name in use:

"1691, May 24. Christened Hadasa, daughter of Arthur Richardson.

"1693, Sep. 4. Christened John, son of Nicholas and Hadassah Davis."—St. Dionis Backchurch.

In the Lancashire "Church Surveys," 1649-1655, being the first volume of the Lancashire and Cheshire Record Society's publications, edited by Colonel Fishwick, occur Thurston Brown, Thurston Brere, Thurston Brich, on one single page of the index.

To tell a lie is to tell a lee in Lancashire.

Several names seem to have been taken directly from the Hebrew tongue. "Amalasioutha" occurs as a baptismal name in the will of a man named Corbye, 1594 (Rochester Wills); Barijirehah in that of J. Allen, 1651, and Michalaliel among the Pilgrim Fathers (Hotten).

Colonel Cunningham, in his annotations of the "Alchemist," says, speaking of the New Englanders bearing the Puritan prejudices with them: "So deeply was it rooted, that in the rebellion of the colonies a member of that State seriously proposed to Congress the putting down of the English language by law, and decreeing the universal adoption of the Hebrew in its stead."—Vol. ii. p. 33, Jonson's Works.

The following entry is a curiosity:

"1756, May 24. Buried Love Venus Rivers."—St. Peter, Cornhill.

Even Nathaniel may have been a pre-Reformation name, for Grumio says, "Call forth Nathaniel, Joseph, Nicholas, Philip, Walter, Sugarsop, and the rest; let their heads be sleekly combed" ("Taming of the Shrew," Act iv. sc. 1.), where he is manifestly using the old names.

Zachary was the then form of Zachariah, as Jeremy of Jeremiah. Neither is a nickname.

The story of Cain and Abel would be popularized in the "mysteries." Abelot was a favourite early pet form (vide "English Surnames," index; also p. 82).

"Jan, 1537. Item: payed to Blaze for brawdering a payre of sleves for my lady's grace, xxs."—"Privy Purse Expenses, Princess Mary."

Philip is found just as frequently for girls as boys:

"1588, March 15. Baptized Phillip, daughter of John Younge.

"1587, Feb. 7. Baptized Phillip, daughter of James Laurence."—St. Columb Major.

In the Oxford edition, 1859, is a foot-note: "Appoline was the usual name in England, as Appoline in France, for Apollonia, a martyr at Alexandria, who, among other tortures, had all her teeth beaten out."

Mr. Beesley, in his "History of Banbury" (p. 456), curiously enough speaks of this Epiphany as a Puritan example. I need not say that a Banbury zealot would have as soon gone to the block as impose such a title on his child.

Gawain, Gawen, or Gavin lingered till last century in Cumberland and the Furrness district. The surname of Gunson in the same parts shows that "Gun" was a popular form. Hence, in the Hundred Rolls, Matilda fil. Gunne or Eustace Gunnson. The London Directory forms are Gowan, Gowen, and Gowing:

"1593, Nov. 7. Buried Sarra Bone, wife of Gawen Bone."—St. Dionis Backchurch.

A good instance of the position in society of Jane and Joan is seen in Rowley's "A Woman never Vexed," where, in the dramatis personæ, Jane is daughter to the London Alderman, and Joan servant-wench to the Widow. The play was written about 1630.

There seems to have been some difficulty in forming the feminines of Charles, all of which are modern. Charlotte was known in England before the queen of George III. made it popular, through the brave Charlet la Trémouille, Lady Derby; but it was rarely used:

"1670, Oct. 26. Sir Saml. Morland to Carola Harsnet."—Westminster Abbey.

"1703. Charlotte Eliza, d. of Mr. John Harmand, a French minister."—Hammersmith.

"9 Will. III. June 29. Caroletta Hasting, defendant."—Decree Rolls, MSS. Record Office.

Carolina, Englished into Caroline, became for a while the favourite, but Charlotte ran away with the honours after the beloved princess of that name died.

Bethia still lingers in certain families, but its origin has manifestly been forgotten. In Notes and Queries, February 23, 1861, Mr. W. A. Leighton deems the name an incorrect version of the scriptural Bithiah (1 Chron. iv. 18); while "G.," writing March 9, 1861, evidently agrees with this conclusion, for after saying that his aunt, a sister, and two cousins bear it, he adds, "They spell it Bethia and Bathia, instead of Bithiah, which is the accurate form"! Miss Yonge also is at fault: "The old name of Bethia, to be found in various English families, probably came from an ancestral Beth on either Welsh, Scots, or Irish sides." She makes it Keltic.

The latest instance of Bethia I have seen is the following, on a mural tablet in Kirkthorpe Church, York:—

"Bethia Atkins, ob. Ap. 16th, 1851, aged 74."

"But the ridicule which falls on this mode of naming children belongs not to these times only, for the practice was in use long before."—Harris, "Life of Oliver Cromwell," p. 342.

This child was buried a few days later. From the name given the father seems to have expected the event.

From 1585 to 1600, that is, in fifteen years, Warbleton register records more than a hundred examples of eccentric Puritanism.

This name crept into Yorkshire after Accepted Frewen became archbishop. "Thornton Church is a little episcopal chapel-of-ease, rich in Nonconformist monuments, as of Accepted Lister, and his friend Dr. Hale."—Mrs. Gaskell's "Charlotte Brontë," p. 37.

Faith-my-joy was buried June 12, 1602. While the name was Puritan in the sense that it would never have been given but for the zealots, it was merely a translation of the Purefoy motto, "Pure Foi ma Joi." Antony turned it into a spiritual allusion.

"On Jan. 28, 17 James I., William Foster ... together with Sir Henry Burton, Susan Mowne, and James Bynde, and Sanctia or Sence his wife, joined in conveying to Robert Raunce and Edward Thurland ... a house and land in Carshalton on trust to sell."—"Bray's Surrey," ii. 513.

Erasmus became a popular baptismal name, and still exists:

"1541, Jan. 3. Baptized Erasmus, sonne of John Lynsey."—St. Peter, Cornhill.

"1593, Sep. 16. Baptized Erasmus, sonne of John Record, merchaunt tailor."—Ditto.

"1611, July 18. Buried Erasmus Finche, captaine, of Dover Castle."—Cant. Cath.

"April 6, 1879, at St. Peter's Thanet, entered into rest, Mary Given Clarke, aged 71 years."—Church Times, April 10, 1879.

The following is curious, although it does not properly belong to this class:

"1629, July 11. Baptized Subpena, a man childe found at the Subpena office in Chancery Lane."—St. Dunstan.

Melior was a favourite:—

"1675, April 15. Baptized Melior, d. of Thomas and Melior Richardson."—Westminster Abbey.

"1664-5, Feb. 22. William Skutt seeks renewal of a wine licence, which he holds in behalf of his mother-in-law, Melior Allen, of Sarum, at £10 a year."—"C. S. P. Dom."

"1552, July 11. Baptized Mellior, d. of John James."—St. Columb Major.

"1661, Sep. 6. Baptized Faith Dionis, Charity Dionis, Grace Dionis, three foundlings."—St. Dionis, Backchurch.

The Manchester Evening Mail, March 22, 1878, says, "At Stanton, near Ipswich, three girls, having been born at one birth, were baptized Faith, Hope, and Charity."

Constance had been an old English favourite, its nick and pet forms being Cust, or Custance, or Cussot (vide "English Surnames," p. 67, 2nd edition). The Puritan dropped these, but adopted "Constant" and "Constancy." The more worldly, in the mean time, curtailed it to "Con."

Sophia did not come into England for a century after this. But, while speaking of Greek names, the most popular was Philadelphia:

"1639, May 3. Buried the Lady Philadelphia Carr."—Hillingdon, Middlesex.

"1720, Aug. 6. Married William Adams and Philadelphia Saffery."—Cant. Cath.

"1776, Jan. 5. Buried Philadelphia, wife of John Read."—Blockley, Glouc.

Whether Penn styled the city he founded after the Church mentioned in the Apocalypse, or after a friend or kinswoman, or because, interpreted, it was a Quaker sentiment, I cannot say. But Philadelphia, in James I.'s reign, had become such a favourite that I have before me over a hundred instances, after no very careful research. None was needed; it appears in every register, and lingered on into the present century.

"1658. Mr. Charles Beswicke, minister of the parish ch. of Stockport, and Sylance Symonds, d. of Mr. Robert Symonds, of Daubever, co. Derby, published March 28, April 4 and 11, 1658."—Banns, Parish Church, Stockport.

This Silence was either mother or grandmother to Silence Thyer, but I am not sure which is the relationship. If grandmother, then there must have been three generations of "Silences."

"I myself have known some persons in London, and other parts of this kingdom, who have been christened by the names of Faith, Hope, Charity, Mercy, Grace, Obedience, Endure, Rejoice, etc."—Brome's "Travels in England," p. 279.

Repentance lingered longer than I thought. In the churchyard of Mappowder, Dorset, is a tombstone to the memory of "Repentance, wife of," etc. She died within the last twenty years. There is no doubt that these names found their latest home in Devon and Dorset. The names in Mr. Blackmore's novels corroborate this.

This is another case of a Puritan name that got into high society. Accepted Frewen died an archbishop; Humble Ward became first Baron Ward. His daughter Theodosia married Sir Thomas Brereton, Bart.

"Faithful Teate was minister at Sudbury, Suffolk, at the time Richard Sibbes, who was born close by, was growing up."—Sibbes' Works, 1. xxvi. Nichol, 1862.

Antony à Wood says Robert Abbott, minister at Cranbrook, Kent, published a quarto sermon in 1626, entitled "Be-thankful London and her Sisters." When we remember that Warbleton in 1626 had at least a dozen Be-Thankfuls among its inhabitants, and that Cranbrook was within walking distance, we see where the title of this discourse was got.

Live-well Chapman was a Fifth Monarchy man. There is still extant a pamphlet headed "A Declaration of several of the Churches of Christ, and Godly People, in and about the City of London, concerning the Kingly Interest of Christ, and the Present Sufferings of His Cause, and Saints in England. Printed for Live-well Chapman, 1654."

These two were twins:

"1589, Oct. 12. Baptized Fre-gyft and Fear-not, ye children of John Lulham."—Warbleton.

This, no doubt, will be a relative of the well-known Puritan, Comfort Starr, born in the adjacent hamlet of Ashford.

A tablet in Northiam Church says—

"In memory of Thankfull Frewen, Esq., patron of, and a generous benefactor to, this Church: who was many years purse-bearer and afterwards secretary to Lord Keeper Coventry, in the reign of Charles the First."

A flat stone in the chancel commemorates the second Thankful:

"Hic situs est vir reverendus Thankfull Frewen hujus ecclesiæ per quinquaginta sex annos rector sanctissimus & doctissimus ... obiit 2do Septembris, 1749, anno ætatis 81mo."

We have already seen that Stephen Vynall had a daughter baptized No-merit at Warbleton, September 28, 1589. Heley's influence followed him to Isfield, as this entry proves.

"1723.—Welthiana Bryan."—Nicholl's "Coll. Top. et Gen.," iii. 250.

Pleasant lasted for some time:

"1757, Jan. 11. Married Thomas Dunn and Pleasant Dadd."—Cant. Cath.

A dozen Freemans may be seen within the limits of half that number of pages in the Finchley registers. Here is one:

"1603, Feb. 26. Baptized Freeman, filius Freeman Page."

That is, he held him crosswise in his arms.

"And here was 'Bartholomew Fayre' acted to-day, which had not been these forty years, it being so satyricall against Puritanism, they durst not till now."—Pepys, Sept. 7, 1661.

That some changed their names for titles of more godly import need not be doubted. William Jenkin says, "I deny not, but in some cases it may be lawfull to change our names, or forbear to mention them, either by tongue or pen: but then we should not be put upon such straits by the badnesse of our actions (as the most are) which we are ashamed to own, but by the consideration of God's glory, or the Churches good, or our own necessary preservation in time of persecution."—"Exposition of Jude," 1652, p. 7.

A child was baptized, January 10, 1880, in the parish church of Stone, near Dartford, by the name of Sou'wester. He was named after an uncle who was born at sea in a south-westerly gale, who received the same name (Notes and Queries, February 7, 1880).

We have already recorded Hate-evil as existing in the Banbury Church register.

The practice of hyphening names, as a condition of accepting property, etc., is of recent origin. By this means not a double baptismal, but a double patronymic, name is formed. But though manifestly increasing, the number of such double surnames is not yet a large one.

"At Faversham a tradesman in 1847 had a son baptized Church-reform, and wished for another, to style him No-tithes, but wished in vain."—P. S. in Notes and Queries, February 3, 1866.

Sometimes, however, one was deemed enough, as, for instance, "Charitye, daughter of the Lord knows who!" This is from Youlgreave, Derbyshire, but the correspondent of Notes and Queries does not give the date.

Made in the USA
Coppell, TX
30 November 2022

87442239R00079